MANIFESTATIONS OF GOD FOR AND THROUGH ME

Corine V. SOLOMON

Clever Fox PUBLISHING
Chennai • Bangalore

CLEVER FOX PUBLISHING
Chennai, India

Published by CLEVER FOX PUBLISHING 2025

ISBN: 978-93-6707-961-4

DEDICATION

"To the Triune God - Father, Son, and Holy Spirit - I dedicate this labor of love, 'Manifestations of God for and true me.' Born out of obedience to the gentle whisper of the Holy Spirit, this book is a testament to the transformative power of Your presence in my life. May it be a reflection of Your glory, a declaration of Your goodness, and a tribute to the unfathomable love that compels me to share my true testimonies with the world. With all intentions that it bring glory, honor, and praise to Your eternal throne, now and forevermore."

Acknowledgement

"I would like to extend my deepest gratitude tc my loving husband, who has been patient and understanding throughout my struggles in writing this book.

I am also grateful to my granddaughter, Samanta Solomon Wrights, for her help and support. Special thanks go to my helpers, Larisa L. Kelly and Roy L. Ebanks, who have assisted me in overcoming the technology challenges I faced. Most importantly, I want to once more express my heartfelt thanks to Father God for guiding me through it all and providing me with such a wonderful support system."

Contents

Introduction xi

1. "A Man At the Door" 1
2. "A View on a Bit of the Future" 3
3. "The Water Fountain" 5
4. "A Christmas Gift for Nelly" 8
5. "Poisoned" 10
6. "Jacqueline's Healings" 12
7. "Timmy's Dog" 15
8. "Geoffrey's Second Gift" 18
9. "Our Son Healed from Rheumatic Fever" 20
10. "Timmy's Broken Pelvis" 24
11. "Pink Eye" 28
12. "Why a Rubber Band?" 30
13. "Given both to God" 32
14. "An Eye Infection" 35
15. "A Bible Study" 38
16. "But I asked you Father" 42

17. "Called a Witch" 46

18. "Dislocated Foot" 49

19. "A great Nudged by the Spirit" 51

20. "Fornication Exposed" 53

21. "Hurricane Warning" 55

22. "My Mother-in-law's Choice" 57

23. "Gifts for the Children" 60

24. "Nineteen Eighty-six Revival in Savannah" 63

25. "Attacked in Broad Daylight" 67

26. "An Old Galleon" 69

27. "A Big Frog" 71

28. "Healed from Tumors" 75

29. "A Black Fist" 79

30. "Food for Thanks Giving Day" 83

31. "A Message from Hell" 86

32. "He is not the One for You" 90

33. "Attacked by Strokes" 92

34. "A Vivid Short Story" 94

35. "After Nine Plus Years" 96

36. "Needing Carpenter Help" 99

37. "Cayman Airways will Fly to Honduras." 101

38. "A Message to two Brothers" 103

39. "A message for a Sister" 108
40. "Even a Dress and a Pin." 110
41. "Six Coconut Candies" 112
42. "A Knock on my Room Door" 114
43. "Turn Left, Turn Your Head." 117
44. "Results of the Faith of a Lad" 119
45. "A word of Knowledge" 121
46. "A Pauper for a Night" 123
47. "Why and Who?" 127
48. "Search for Casta" 129
49. "My Three Visitors" 132
50. "Who, Lord?" 134
51. "A Three-in-one Blessing" 137
52. "A Whisper in my Ear" 141
53. "My Awesome Fall" 143
54. "My Dads Departure Foretold" 146
55. "I Didn't Know" 151
56. "Another Attack from the Spirit of Hate" 154
57. "Kidney Problem" 158
58. "The Third or Seventh Heaven?" 160
59. "How and Why?" 163
60. "A Spirit of Hate" 166

61. "A Miracle for a Sinner" 169
62. "A Brush with Death" 173
63. "Angels on Amtrak" 175
64. "Born for a Great Purpose" 182
65. "Fought to Live" 187
66. "Five Days of Rain" 189
67. "Incest" 192
68. "A Miracle off a Highway" 194
69. "The Death of a Q C" 196
70. "My Brush with Death" 199
71. "Three Warnings" 202
72. "When God Says No" 204
73. "Curious to see Satan" 207
74. "Helper Beguiled" 210
75. "A Secret" 214
76. "Why me?" 216

Introduction

Dear Reader,

As you journey through the testimonies shared in this collection, subtitled *"Manifestations of God for and Through Me,"* I want to make it clear that every account of God's power manifested, as mentioned in these testimonies, is true. I call upon God, our Creator, as my witness to this truth.

Why are these testimonies only now being written? I can imagine this question being asked – and I assure you, dear reader, you are not alone in this inquiry. I, too, have wrestled with the same question. However, I find comfort in the answer I received in my spirit: *"There is a time for everything."* And so, this is the only response I can offer to anyone who wonders.

If my memory serves me well, the call to write and publish these experiences was brought to my awareness in the latter part of 2021. I recall it being in the month of October, early one morning before dawn.

I firmly believe this was done by the Holy Spirit; and I am almost sure that long before you have finished reading these true testimonies you will agree with me that it would only be The Holy Spirit that was instructing me to do so, but not withstanding this blessing: I do sincerely regret having neglected keeping my Diary up to date, for if I had I would be able to give precise dates, but let me not be so hard on myself as for quite many a Years Life have been throwing some curbed Balls in my path

-large enough to take me off the track, but all thanks and praise to God He keep me footed in Him.

Many a times in Prayer -especial in the early hours of the morning which at such hours I always spend alone in worship/devotion in one form or the other, be it prayer and the reading of The Word, or Prayer and listening to the reading of The Word or any other form that are pleasing to God -one morning in October 2021 before day as always I got out of bed and went to my Lazy-boy chair for worship/devotion and as always I engaged in Prayer and there-in I started complain to Father with bitter tears and deep regret and began seeking forgiveness -for having not -in the many years that I have been saved -accomplished anything that brought glory to His name, this said thought I had many a times before with tears of regret but always this would be short lived as wave of comfort moved over my Soul, but that Morning of October 2021 mentioned above I was up for my alone time with God -sitting in my Lazy Boy of which I always use of what I call: my sitting Alter, before commencing in Prayer this Morning I gazed through the darkness of my Bedroom at the open door which leads to my Bathroom -I then caught sight of the reflection from the night light in my bathroom -which is constantly portrayed on the Tiled wall that conceals the view of my bath tub -the little light seems to always battle with the darkness which in golfs my bedroom -of which I enjoys being in as I spend some quiet time alone in worshiping/devotion to God.

After Prayer that Morning, as I stretched myself out to meditate and relax -in hopes of getting a nap before the Sun or my husband arose but suddenly I became once again burdened with that thought of having not ever done anything to glorify Gods name, then quickly my soul was seemly crushed with sadness, and I began to Cry uncontrollably -using the manual control of the Lazy Boy to a sitting position and slipped myself to the edge of the seat position myself with my head between my knees in tears and great sadness -and with what seemed to be a gentle move or stir I felt the presence of someone standing cape-in-corner slightly off to my right in front of me I had no desire to see who or what it was, and even if I did; -I knew that I was unable to look up but slowly I became aware that it was a familiar presence, I closed my eyes and soon I was relaxed and at a gentle but good paste Memory of things that had taking place in my life throughout the pass years flooded my mind one after the other in gentle whispers-of course at the off start I did not recall them as being of the pass, these acts was being shared with me at a good paçe yet far too fast for me to have written them down -at that time I was highly conscious -as like many times before, that there was with me -what my Mom would say when I shared with her such my experiences as a child. "That's your invisible friend." She would say. Yes -He was, is, and I trust to be with me always, as I often ask Him. Thank the Lord I am constantly aware of His presence.

In that Morning visitation I was shewn, admonished, comforted, and reminded that I did many things for The Kingdom. "O Father I did not remember you doing all this for and through me" I said. Then I heard the whisper to write and publish them. "But Father -not everyone can read'. I whispered back. instantly I heard the words: Audio Book, and then a deep desire of wanting that all people be enable to read this book.

When those shower of Heavenly Rain had pass I regained the strength to recompose myself in the Chair reaching over to the night table on my right I took my large yellow writing pad and pen and wrote a title to every act that I was reminded of.

Much time has passed since those shower of Heavenly blessing fell that Morning -and I have just got started on this assignment, honestly I was a bit hesitant on approaching using my computer as I had not became very familiar with it, before sickness of myself and also a much longer ordeal of sickness of my husband began which threw my life into deep despair, along with all of my other responsibilities in having to earn an honest living for both of us -by controlling our small renting business flooded my path and added to my delay in I getting started.

Then in the early Morning of my second day of being admission to Shetty Hospital for treatment for H. pylori which took place on January 26, 2022, I got out of bed in the early hours of the morning and sat beside a window in effort to engage in my morning devotion, I was once again reminded of this writing assignment -and was there again reminded of more acts that had taking place in the pass and they too was added to those of the previous list which was revealed to me in 2021 after the reminder I made record of them -this time in 'Note' on my cell Phone, as I had not writing material.

I thank God I have now -though to me late -been blessed to get started, and by God's grace I will accomplish it for the Glory of His name, and for which I believe will aid in bringing an extension to His Kingdom.

I wish to share with anyone that have not experienced, recognized, or acknowledged the power of God, and also right here encourage and remind those that have -That He is still the same ALMIGHTY God the faithful one, and He will always be.

Delight yourself in Him and He will give you the desires of your heart. Psalms 37: 4.

And may I remind us that He promised: Never to leave us or forsake us.

Corine V Solomon

"A Man At the Door"

I guess I was almost eight years old or so, and from the time I could remember, I would become scared as soon as the sun set.

I was a bit late for supper one evening, and my mom had left my food in the outside kitchen, which we used to call the Cook-a-rum. Twilight was settling in, and darkness was quickly approaching. My dad was not home, and my mom had already retreated to her room. One of my half-sisters, who was staying with us, and her fiancé were in the pantry spending their allotted time together. I wasn't sure where my brothers were.

Who would accompany me to the kitchen? I considered it, but I knew that unless my brother Watson was present, I had only two choices: go alone or do without.

Not only did I crave the delicious offerings in the kitchen, but I found myself desperately needing them and well knew that the longer I took to move the darker it would get, so I moved outside fast with all intention to grab what I was going for, and get back into the house.

As I headed back from the kitchen door -I did not even remember that I ever was fearful, so I found myself taking my time back to the house, nearing the back door I saw a man standing on the entrance felt of the back door with his back to the wall with his left foot resting on the first step, in his right hand he held a white stick which I would guess was about six or so inches long, with a light like fine burning coals on the tip of it -that was I guess about an inch and a half long, reaching the step -I noticed how the light from our kerosene lamp that was on a shelf witch was on the wall near the door -penetrated the screen of the inner door, and just then the man spoke to me, I looked at him; and he said: "Tell your sister not to marry that man as he will treat her bad."

I walked up the steps confidently and, after closing the screen door, I called my sister's name. I relayed the message from the man without mentioning his presence, and I didn't recall my feelings toward her fiancé.

When hearing the message that I delivered to her she yelled out for mom saying: "Mom you better call this little old Corine." Mom called me and asked: "What is it that you doing now Corine?" I did not reply; and my sister, or her intended did not say anything, and mom did not make any farther investigation.

My sister's father married her off to that tall, dark, handsome young man. Despite the hellish life he gave her, she bore him a daughter and a son.

Let us take note: that from way back God used little children.

Experienced and written by: Corine V. Solomon

"A View on a Bit of the Future"

I was just about ten years old when I was given a Dream, something that have always been very rear in my life, and usually those that is of substances always come before day in the morning just like the one I will share in this testimony where God gave me a view of a bit of the future.

I dreamt I was in our backyard, between my parents' house and the kitchen. I saw myself in a small room with a large glass jar filled with clear water, in which an unborn baby was developing. Suddenly, I was shown a road cutting through Mr. Willie Farrington's vacant land opposite our home, I was then informed about a program that could type whatever we said.

The Road Stadium Drive is right there in West Bay just as I saw in that Dream.

One day, I remember it being in 1998 when my husband brought me a program called Dragon. He was so excited about what this program could do for me. He said, "All you have to do is install it and talk to it. Whatever you want to write, it will type it for you."

What is the baby growing in a Jar -is it happening, or is it yet to come? Will I see this, I am not sure but I believe that whatever God have started he will complete.

I cannot say that I know when such will be, but I believe it will. -May God have mercy on our power hungry, Money greed, human soul-destroying agents of Satan.

Why did God show me these three, does He have any other reason than just for me to see them?

One thing I know: He does all things well.

Experienced and written by: Corine V. Solomon

"The Water Fountain"

A few years after my conversion, I heard a sermon on sanctification at a yearly convention that intrigued me. I realized I wanted this second work of grace in my life, so I began seeking God through prayer. Although I had learned about fasting and tried to incorporate it into my routine, my responsibilities as a parent to four children made it challenging.

I prayed and fasted for a few Months, of which I believe was about three.

I remember one Saturday when my husband was at home. He spent the day doing some much-needed woodworking in the backyard, setting up his electric saw. The children were all engaged in whatever activities captured their interest in the yard as well.

I continued with my house chores, between the noise from the saw, hammering, and the joyful noises from the children, I was very alert.

Finally I became overwhelmed by the noise -of which I have never been too tolerant with and by then I was also becoming tired, which was mostly in my lower back and Legs -which is where I have always first felt tiredness, so I retreated to my Daughter's Bedroom, and rested across her Bed in a cape-in corner position with a small pillow under my Head, and rested my left arm over my forehead which helps to bring relaxation to my Body, still being fully conscious of the noises my family were still engaged in somewhat interfered with my effort to relax, but I tried to make the best of the situation, when slowly I sensed a Peace and calm drift into the Bedroom and seemly rested over me relaxing my entire body -yes I could still here that my family was in the back yard, but their activities had no effect on me.

I lay there just enjoying the Peace and profound calm that had entered the Bedroom and settled over me, which at that time I was not aware of what was taking place.

From what I thought was the mattress I was lying on, a crystal-clear water fountain rose beside me. Instead of water, it turned to fire as it descended through my body.

That fire did not burn like the normal fire, but it had an effect on my body -of which I am unable to explain, yet there and then I knew the work that it had performed within me, but still the thoughts of it troubled my mind, and with it brought doubts of what I knew, and in truth from that day I saw great changes in my spiritual life, for one: I had more strength to resist Temptation of sin in whatever form it presented itself.

I kept what happened in my daughter's room that Saturday to myself for weeks before sharing it with my husband. After a couple of months, I visited a local elder, a pastor, to discuss my experience. When I described it, he asked for my thoughts. I explained that I was cautious about how to interpret it, which is why I sought his guidance. He then asked if I felt sanctified or was seeking sanctification.

I shared with him that I had been asking God to sanctify me.

He then said: "well it sounds to me like God was showing you that He was sanctifying you.

I thanked him for the reconfirmation and left rejoicing and with a greater determination to live to please God.

Experienced and experienced by: Corine V. Solomon

"A Christmas Gift for Nelly"

Nelly's family consisted of eight members: the parents, three boys, and three girls. Nelly, the youngest girl and the last child, was still very young when their mother passed away sometime earlier that year.

Nelly and I became closer after her mom passed away. We even gave each other new names: I was Abna, and she was Choheadna, which sounded like "Cow-head." I didn't realize how unusual those names were at the time.

I just recalled one day -I would say; about two Years after her mother had passed, and like many days before I went to spend time with Nelly at her home, I walked around the back of the house as always and calling for her -of course by her new name.

"Who are you looking for, who is Choheadna?"a female voice asked. I am looking for Nelly." I replied, "well call her by her right name not Choheadna." It was then that I learned that a strange woman was in their home -this woman was a friend of her father and he had brought her in their home to be their new mother.

There is so much I could share about our friendship through the years. However, the purpose of this testimony is the same as all the others: to give thanks to God and bring glory to His name. Praise His holy name He works in mysterious ways and performs His wonders.

One night that year, I was sitting in our family room beside the front screen door -awaiting my mother to return to her sawing machine as she was that night, like she was almost every night -sewing clothes for our neighbors for Christmas.

Just before my mother returned to the room, I heard a very familiar voice call my name -yes it was the voice of Nelly's mother, it asked me to see that Nelly get something good for Christmas, her voice so clear that her presents seem to be standing outside our front door, I felt that if I looked, I would have seen her, but being younger I was scared to do so.

I am persuaded that -that was my first call to start a donation ministry, although I was just a child.

Thank God Nelly did get something good for Christmas.

Experienced and experienced by: Corine V. Solomon

"Poisoned"

My seventh birthday had just passed when I began experiencing severe abdominal pains. After several days of complaining, my mother finally took me to Nurse Lue's house, where a tall, elderly English doctor named Dr. Horter was holding his clinic.

After thoroughly examining me, he told my mother that the pains I was experiencing were due to worms. Rising from his seat, he walked to the other side of the room, speaking to her as he moved. He explained that he would give her one capsule, and she must make sure I took it early in the morning before eating breakfast.

He took two dark brown bottles of different sizes from the cupboard. From the larger one, he carefully removed something that looked like a pimpled berry and dropped it into the smaller bottle. Then he pulled out a flat bottle that appeared to be nearly filled with water. About an inch and a half from the bottom, a white, powdery substance had settled, looking like some kind of mysterious residue.

Shaking it violently, I noticed that the stuff in the bottle was all white, did I hear him tell Mom that she was to give it to me or?... I do not recall, but I do remember that it tasted like Peppermint.

The following morning, Mom woke me up and told me it was time to take my worm medicine. She handed me a glass of water and, holding out her other hand, showed me the capsule— a small, purple, pimpled berry-looking thing between her fingers. "Put it in your mouth," she said, "but don't bite it—just swallow. I shrank back, telling her that I could not drink it because it would poison me.

Poison, what did that word mean? I was not sure; I was only saying what I heard.

Mom threatened me that if I did not drink it, she would give me a whooping, so I sure knew it was better for me to take my chance with that Purple pimpled berry she was forcing me to drink.

The third morning after I drank that purple berry mom gazed at me and said, "My God you are as yellow as Gold." Then she rushed me back to Dr. Horter, who told her that the *chillepolum* had poisoned my liver and that I had developed yellow jaundice.

"My God! she told me that it would Poison her; and I forced her to drink it."

Many adults have been warned of God through little children-some listen, some do not.

Experienced and written by: Corine V. Solomon

"Jacqueline's Healings"

At that time, our only biological daughter, Jacqueline, was Nine years old. She was always the first to be ready for school and was on standby to help her brothers get ready, ensuring they could all leave on time with their dad, who handled most of their transportation to and from school. During that time, everyone was enrolled at the vibrant and inspiring Truth for Youth School.

I'm not sure which day of the week it was when the incident I'm about to share took place, but I clearly remember being in the younger boy's bedroom, helping the youngest get ready for school. At that moment, Jacqueline walked in and told me she was experiencing pain in her side. Looking at her, I could see that she was in agony.

I helped her lay down on a lower bunk bed and asked where the pain was. When she pointed, I pressed on the spot, and she flinched. I then performed the "pull up the right leg" test and noticed she struggled to straighten it, which made me suspect an appendicitis attack, similar to what I had experienced with her dad early in our marriage.

I couldn't remember if I used a wet or ice cloth, but I encouraged her to pray for help. She closed her eyes as I led in prayer, and I knew she had learned to pray quietly from her heart to God.

After the prayer, she turned on her side and fell asleep. She woke up before her dad left to take the boys to school, asking if he had already gone.

No, they are just about to leave.

"Ma, I'm going to school too," she said, heading towards the front door. "Are you sure you feel good enough to go, Love?" I called to her, "Yes, Ma, I am fine; all the pain is gone." She said as she hurried to get into her dad's vehicle. Praise God He blessed my Family once more and increased my Faith in Him.

Last night after retiring from writing of God's healing touch on my daughter Jacqueline with the Appendix attack, I got a thinking how short the record of her healing had been -and just then in a quiet voice I heard The Spirit whisper: "What about the lump she had in her Brest?"

"Thank you, Holy Spirit," I replied as I made plans to also share God's blessing in writing on it and asked Him to please remind me of it in the Morning. well Though I am a bit late on getting started, I am thankful I was Reminded.

It was early one Monday morning as I entered the Kitchen when Jacqueline, who was almost fourteen Years old then, exited her bedroom informing me that there was a lump in her left Breast, I examined it; and found that it was about the size of a medium size Marble also as hard as one.

My first thought to aid her was to get some butter and Pot Salt, I rubbed them together until all the salt had been rubbed fine, an old remedy told to me by my grandmother Matilda. I rubbed her entire breast clockwise and anticlockwise with it, then we paused and prayed placing the Problem in God's hands. After the rubbing and Prayer, her discomfort was settled, and she went off to school.

The next day as she made ready for school, she learned that the lump was no longer in her Brest.

Yes -I am still learning about the works of God and -I trust be doing so for as long as I live, know: He still does healing and Miracles.

I am right now hearing deep in my being, "greater things than this I will do through you"

Experienced and written by: Corine V. Solomon

"Timmy's Dog"

When my children were young, they always wanted to pet any dogs, cats, or birds they encountered. They often longed for pets of their own, but I told them they wouldn't be allowed to have any until they were old enough and learned how to care for them. I can honestly say I was fortunate to have to repeat this message only a few times.

When our eldest son Timothy whom we call Timmy was about eight or nine years old one day on his return from school he came to me with an exciting story about Eddie Arch and his mother dog with all the beautiful Pups she had, I listened attentively as he described each Pup and felt assured that I knew the question that would come next – well I was wrong that time but about six or seven weeks later after school he came to me with a similar story and began by telling me that he was a big boy now, and was willing and able to care for a pet assuring me that if I would allow him to get a little dog -then quickly he began to share his strategy on caring for a pet, then he pleaded my approval.

I recalled telling him that I would think about it, a few evenings later on his return from school he came to me all excited informing me that he had asked Eddie for one of the Pups, and that he said yes if your parent agreed to you having it, and without any reply from me he proceeded to tell me all about the love between himself and the Pup and once again began to plead my approval.

I told him that his Dad and I had agreed to allow him to have a Pet, so since his choice was a dog, he may bring the pup home with an understanding that its full care was upon him, and that if he fails on this agreement the pet will be taken from him and giving away.

I do not believe that Timmy slept well that night.

The next day he entered the house with a bundle of Brown hair in his arms, entering my room where I was sitting on my bed, he placed the beautiful, plump, six week pup in my lap -looking it over I learned that it was female, and that there was a patch of white hair which began from the back end of its jaws down between her two front legs and covered quite a lot of the inside of them which formed a Cross or a common T.

I hugged the pup as I loved it on sight –"what should I name her Mom?"

He asked. "well she is yours; whatever you would like to name her that will be it." I seeing his dilemma in choosing a name I said as I showed him the T on her breast "Maybe you could name her Tindy" for two reason she is yours, and the T on her Breast.

Timmy was well please with her name, and in a few days she knew it well.

Time flew by, and Tindy had grown into an adult. One morning, just after the children left for school, I met with Tindy and my old gray cat to serve them breakfast in our backyard, a routine I followed every weekday.

One Week day on my way out to feed them Tindy was the first to greet me at the back door, and as I attempted to welcome her greeting by rubbing her head when I notice that her entire top lip was covered with what looked to be long dark breast nipples, and in her eyes I could see that she was very uncomfortable, and that she was asking me for help,

I struggle to fully express my feelings upon seeing her in that condition, especially knowing that there was no medical help available on the island at that time. I couldn't help but wonder, "Will God heal a dog?"

Having been holding their plate of food in my right hand I held the top her head with my left hand and asked God to Please heal her.

After school Timmy and the other children saw the condition of their Dog -I did not here any of them pray for her, but I am almost sure they did as the knowledge of praying they obtained at home and at school.

Any way I comforted them that I had Prayed for her and believed that God would heal her.

And the next morning we all were filled with joy to see our dog healed from those awful things on her Lip -of which we later learned is called Yaws.

Praise God, He heals animals too. Our family has experienced this several times since Tindy, Timmy's dog, was healed.

Experience and written by: Corine Solomon

"Geoffrey's Second Gift"

Geoffrey, my fourth child and my third son, had a challenging journey to this sin-ridden world. It was a rough ride for both of us, but thank God we have finally completed the second part of our journey—his birth.

When he arrived, he was almost like a little skeleton poorly wrapped in his skin which was much too large for him; as he was born sick and had lost a lot of weight before birth, and in his fight to live he had incurred Hernias and asthma -I have shared more of this in another testimony of him titled "Fought to live."

Like many nights before, I found myself in the boy's bedroom to attend to Geoffrey. After we moved him out of our room, he still wasn't well and would have episodes related to his ailments.

Late one night, I was awakened by the sound of his groaning

On my way down the Pantry to their room, I noticed I did not hear him anymore, but thought it best to still check in on them.

Reaching their bedroom I moved the two sandbags which kept their room door ajar, and it was then that I learned that he was still groaning.

After inquiring from him the cause of his honing, I learned that he was thirsty and wished to have a glass of milk, but was afraid to go to the Kitchen alone.

Although I knew that he was old enough to go to the kitchen and get the milk for himself -I went and got the glass of milk for him waited till he was finished that I may tucked him back in bed, and return the glass.

The next evening worship -when it was their time to share what they wished; Geoffrey was the first to speak: "Mom I was wanting to know if you were really a Christian," he paused a bit, and then with his speech; "Do you remember the last night you came and got me a glass of milk from the kitchen?"

"Yes -I do," I replied.

"When you did go to the kitchen mom: I saw a blue light come down from the light over the dining table, and it came and stud in my room door -when you came back with the glass of milk you walked right through the blue light, and when you left you walked right through it again, and it was then that I was shown that you are a Christian.

His testimony answered my curiosity on how and why I was able to hear him honing so lightly from all the way in his bedroom.

Experienced and written by: Corine V. Solomon

"Our Son Healed from Rheumatic Fever"

Our fourth son, Kimbert had not spent many months into his night birthday, when he began to run a fever, for a few days I did all I knew how to do in effort to get him well.

After about three days of treating him for the fever, late one night, I reckoned it was after twelve as I was already asleep and was awoken by a knocking on our room door.

It was Kimbert, he was again suffering from an attack of the fever, which I knew was tremendously high, although I did not have a thermometer.

After treating him with my home remedies, I let him lie between his father and me. However, after a few minutes, the heat from his body became unbearably uncomfortable. Realizing that our proximity would only worsen his fever, I asked his father to fetch a floor bed we had stored in our closit and lay beside our bed for the remaining hours of the night

It was on that very night that Satan was revealed to me—an experience I have shared in another testimony within this book.

We took Kimbert to the Government Hospital the following Morning, seeing that they were not able to get an accurate reading of the fever the doctor interned him right away, anticipating that he would be in hospital a long time if he survived the night as his blood test revealed that he was under a bad attacked of Rheumatic fever -what limited medication they had back then was administered.

Due to the fever, he would often drift off to sleep, and at the hospital, he once again fell into a deep, weakened sleep—a state I assumed was brought on by the intensity of the fever.

The doctor informed us that they would do their best with what treatments they had, but needed us to understand that if he survived the fever, he would most likely have a weak heart or possibly become an invalid.

I told the doctor that we would leave all of his future up to the decision of our creator.

When I heard the devastating news, I prayed even more, asking God to heal him—again. Years earlier, he and his brother Ellio had survived a deadly virus that claimed the lives of several children on the island.

Before that illness, I had read a testimony from a Christian sister in the U.S. She had been barren and pleaded with God for a son. Her prayers were answered, but at age seven, her son fell gravely ill. God told her three times He would take him, but she insisted on his healing. The boy survived, but later got into serious trouble—crime, prison, and eventually died by electrocution at 21.

She ended her testimony with a plea: do not force the hand of God, for it may bring sorrow.

After reading that sister's testimony I made a promise to never force the hand of God.

During this illness, I prayed for their healing and told God that I wanted my boys to be healed—if it was His will, and if their lives would bring glory to His name. But if not, though it would hurt deeply to let them go, I still desired His will to be done in my life, even through pain. I thank God that the very next morning, both of them were completely healed.

Now Kimbert was sick again, and I was back on the Potter's wheel and again as much as it seems to tear my heart in pieces -I repeated the same prayer often each day -for him just as I had done when he and Ellio were sick.

Two nights and almost another day Kimbert was still in Hospital with hardly responding to anyone or action, still running the hot fever -I sat in a chair at the head of his bed just commuing with God from my heart to His, when I saw that Kimbert had roll on his right side facing me, opening his eyes he said: "Mama, are you still going to publish one of your books?" "Yes, Bo," I replied with much joy in my heart and hope for his full recovery.

"Would you publish It's Who mama?" he inquired. "I sure will, Bo."

This little book "Its Who," was a bedtime story that I had written for him as a reward for the good grades he had earned in school.

The doctor made his rounds that morning around ten O'clock and found that the fever was broken. He said he would keep him for the rest of that day and overnight, and if he remained fever- free, he would be discharged the next day. Thank God, I was able to take him home the next day.

The medical team did not voice their surprise at Kimbert's speedy recovery -at least not that I heard but thank God the eyes is the light of the body and the thought of the heart is revealed by our countenance.

Brethren, family, and friends, I admonish you to please put your trust in God. I agree that at times it may seem like God is long in answering your prayer, but I can assure you, he is never late, but always on time, and that he does all things right.

See, he cannot go back on His promises as He honors His word more than He does His name.

Therefore you can trust God always.

Experienced and written by: Corine V Solomon

"Timmy's Broken Pelvis"

Today Is March 31, 2022. Wow! How fast the Years have passed, this incident I will share here took place in 1979 -Timothy, my first Child and the Eldest of my five sons, was fourteen Years of age then.

One evening around five-thirty, I sent him to the Merren's family supermarket nearby to buy something we needed for the kitchen. He had just left on his new bike—a Christmas gift from his dad—when someone came to the house with shocking news: he had been hit by a car and taken to the hospital, but thankfully, they assured us he was still alive.

I pulled myself away from my duty and hurriedly dressed, asking my husband, who of course was also making ready to get to the Hospital, to hold the fourth down until I returned, then he could go -because having the other Children at home, we both could not leave.

On reaching the hospital room where my son was, the doctor told me that Timmy was all safe, then paused his sentence and, walking towards the door, he requested that I follow him to his office.

As I said, Mrs. Solomon," he began as I entered his office, "your son is all in the clear—except that his pelvis is broken in two places." He moved to sit beside his desk and turned on the X-ray viewer, where Timothy's scan was still displayed. Pointing with his pen to the fractures, he continued, "Because of this, he'll need to be confined to bed on his back for six to eight weeks. He won't be able to sit up, stand, walk, or even turn from side to side on his own. The nursing staff will provide full bed care. So rest assured—he'll be well taken care of here in the hospital.

Have Timothy been informed of this? I inquired.

Being assured that he had informed him, and all the Nursing staff of his damages and had given them all full instruction of the care he would require, I returned to his room to see that all was well with him before I left the Hospital.

His broken bone troubled my mind, but hearing of the long bed confinement he would have to endure for healing added no comfort to the sudden stress that had come my way since hearing of the accident.

"Did the Doctor tell you about the damage you received from the accident?" I inquired from Timothy as I reached the room.

"Yes, Mam, he did," and he went on to tell me all the details including the long bed confinement, of which I could see he was not too please about.

I then prayed with him and did my best to reassure him that everything would be alright. I explained that I had to leave so his dad could visit before the end of visiting hours. With God's blessing, I promised to return at the earliest visiting hour the next day.

I was early for the eleven o'clock visiting time the following day, but the station nurse allowed me to go to Timothy's room.

He was wide awake, lying flat on his back as expected, stretched out to his full length. I greeted him and showed him the drinks and biscuits I had brought. We then chatted about the evening of the accident, which he began by asking about his bicycle. "Well, it only needs a new front wheel—that's what your dad said," I told him.

"Did the Car run over it?" he asked; "No -I was told that when the Car hit you, you and the Bike were flung up into the air about twelve or more feet." Our conversation continued for a while longer.

I kissed him on his forehead as I planned to leave for the day, I asked him if it was anything he wished for me to do for him before I leave – "Yes Mom; I wish for you to pray for me I wish that Jesus heal me," he went on to expressing that he did not wish to lay in bed for as long as the doctor said.

I don't clearly remember if I asked him whether he believed Jesus could heal his broken bone, but knowing myself, I likely did. What I do remember is saying, "OK—so be it," and we prepared to pray.

I placed my hand just above his pelvis and prayed, thanking God for sparing Timothy's life and asking Him, in Jesus' name, to heal the broken bones. As I ended the prayer, I heard in my spirit, "Let him get up and walk to the door and back."

Though I hesitated, knowing the doctor's orders, I felt strongly this was an act of faith. I told Timothy I believed Jesus wanted him to do it, and quietly hoped the nurse wouldn't come in just then.

Timothy got out of bed in slow motion and walked in the said manner to the door, and back into his bed -just as I had instructed him, and through his desire which coincided with what was being spoken then to my spirit at that time -I went and asked the doctor to take another X-Ray of his Pelvic, this I did because of his pleading request.

The Doctor assured me that there was no need to take another X-Ray as one was taken the day before when he was brought into hospital, but promised me that he would do so the following day. I then insisted that he order the X-Ray to be done that day, reluctantly, he ordered the X-Ray to be done this he did so without asking me the reason for my request.

I returned to Timothy's room with the change of my plan to go home, knowing that I needed to know the results of the X-Ray, soon the Porter wheeled Timothy out to the X-Ray department, they had not been gone very long when they returned him to the room, within a short time the doctor summoned me to his office, when I reached his office, he was sitting at his desk staring at the X-Ray.

I stood in the doctor's office for a bit before he acknowledged that I was there – "Oh yes! Mrs. Solomon" he said as he turned in his Chair glancing at me he continued: "Madam I do not understand this X-Ray that was just taking -as it is showing that there is no broken boon, but it was just yesterday the first X-Ray revealed that his Pelvis was broken in two places," he said as he added the previous X-Ray to the light –"see" he said pointing to the first X-Ray, then once again he added the new X-Ray to the light -shaking his head as he gazed there on –"I must perform a physical examination on your son." he added leaving his office, and I followed him to Timothy's room.

After he was finished the examination, he said to me: "You may take your son home, he is well, I will inform the nurse." He added as he walked off in ponder.

I praise God then for His healing touch on Timothy, and I am still praising him now, and I will add: I thank him in advance for the healing touch that He will perform on his spirit, soul, and body in the very near future.

Experienced and written by: Corine V. Solomon

"Pink Eye"

It was 1980, and by now I was the mother of my six birth born children -Five Sons and one Daughter and the stepmother to two adopted daughters.

The new circulating news around the neighborhood on that weekend mid-morning was that an Eye disease called Pink Eye -some call it Red Eye was spreading rapidly through the Island.

This is an awful eye problem that can attack both eyes, and is contagious causing great suffering -I believe it can cause blindness.

I am not very knowledgeable concerning it, but with the blessing of Technology, anyone who has access to it can research it.

Anyway, it began to cause much stress in the family I think it was due to my Parent having had some prior experience with it, and they lived only a few yards away from us.

The news on this began to cause me much concern, especially concerning the health of my children.

I clearly remember when the news reached our home that day—I was in the yard, standing with my back to my parents' house, starting to feel stressed. In that moment, I was gently reminded that God is still our healer. Memories of what I had read in the Bible and witnessed Him do came flooding back.

I then began to pray, asking God to please have mercy on all my family members and cover us with the protective Blood of Jesus from this Eye disease.

Though I couldn't fully grasp the extent of the suffering others on the island were facing, I heard many stories about it. I can't describe it all, but I can truly say this: the pink eye outbreak passed over our family. Praise God, once again He heard and answered my cry for His divine intervention.

Experienced and written by: Corine V. Solomon

"Why a Rubber Band?"

The time for fasting had come again, as I had long learned that some situations in life require more than just prayer—fasting must be added so we can overcome and have victory over whatever challenges arise.

In a Christian's Life praying should be like eating regular meals, some have said. - but from my few years of experience, I have chosen to add a snack in between meals.

As always, I engaged in Prayer and fasting for three days, and as always, my husband, though unsaved at that time, was faithful in filling in for me on my duties, If we had house help or not, which was the case at this time.

I was seeking God for healing of my body and care-taking with our three first sons as my husband was taking me to the United States for medical aid, and my mother was only able to care for our daughter.

Let me mention here that back then in the time of fasting, I did not eat or drink anything whatsoever, not even water -on the third day of my fast, I became very hungry and thirsty, but as always, I never revealed my need to anyone.

After my husband ended his brief visit, I lay on the bed enjoying the cool breeze through the open door. As I finished a quiet prayer, I saw a Mammee Apple—rare and special to us from my native Bay Islands of Honduras—appear in midair, being peeled. Its strong aroma filled the room, quenching all hunger and thirst. The vision faded just as my husband returned, mentioning the scent. I invited him to lie beside me.

As he rested, I saw a large rubber band stretching above the bed. I described it to him, and when it snapped in slow motion, I said, "It is broken." At that moment, we heard a crash from the boys' room. My husband got up to check, but I told him there was no need—it was the enemy reacting, because his plan over our boys had just been broken.

Later, my husband checked out the boys room and all was well.

Somehow the conversation of the Scent of the Mammea Apple and the Rubber band arose between my husband and me.

It was easy to explain the scent of the Mammea Apple, but the vision of the rubber band remains a mystery. I believe it symbolized the breaking of the enemy's plan against us. Why a rubber band? I still don't know. I can only guess, since I find no direct support for it in the Word. Still, I believe that not everything about God and His works can be fully explained, perceived, or understood.

I am glad to say that within days after my fast, all our plans, needs, and desires as of then were all in place. Praise God!!!

Experienced and written by: Corine V. Solomon

"Given both to God"

In about the Year 1976, children of all ages in Cayman were attacked by a very bad Virus. I do not recall that it was given a name, but I recall that it attacked the children with fever, and diarrhea which they did not have long before they would die.

I never heard how many Children died from this Virus, but the sudden death of one little girl —barely two years old—has always stood out in my memory. I remember hearing that her parents rushed her to a hospital in Miami. During the flight, her father believed she had simply fallen asleep in his arms. But when they arrived and he went to lift her over his shoulder, he discovered, to his horror, that she had passed away.

It was not long after the news of the little girl's passing—on a Wednesday morning—that two of our sons, Ellio, who was nearly seven, and Kimbert, almost five, were struck by the same virus. The fever on them was moderate when I left and they had only had a few bowel actions which was far apart -I did my Motherly duties and appointed with my husband concerning caring for the children in my absents as he always did when I had to leave, as Wednesday evenings was the day of the Week for Bible study hosted by Brother Ranford Reid which was held in a large room in the truth for youth school hall.

I was torn between two of my loves that evening -wanted to stay with my Children, and wanting to attend Bible study, knowing that they were in the good hands of their Dad I decided to go to Bible study, as I reached outside my front door my mother called to me from her house which was next door informing me in an excited voice informing me that the Boat of which my father was on was missing.

I do not recall exactly what words of comfort I shared with her, but I know I did the best I could, and went on my way to Bible study; and was in right timing to catch the commencing -as I sat at the table Brother Reid greeted us and said that it was time for Prayer, and that whosoever felt led to Pray must lead in Prayer we all pushed our chairs away from the Table and knelt for Prayer. I was never one that rushed to lead in Prayer; but that evening the contents of my thankful, troubled, burdened Heart spilled and I was the first to start Praying, I am not sure if there was any others that was Praying out, but I well recall that I had not long started to Pray when I felt as if my body was rising from the floor -it was so real that with both hands I held unto my chair, and continued asking for the safety of my Father and the boat crew, and reminded God that He had lone our children to us and that we had given them back to Him, and now two of them were sick, and if He willed to please heal them; but He knowing all things and thereby if they would grow up to live and die a sinful life, and He wished now to take them: I want His will to be done even if it hurts, and to have to part with them would surly hurt.

I realized that making this statement sounded harsh and cruel, but God knows my Heart, and that is still my Prayer to Him concerning them, although they are all now adults.

After Bible study: on reaching home, I went directly to my bathroom to make ready for the Night -I had not been there very long when I was accused in my spirit of not even checking my two sick children.

I stepped through the door that led to the boys' bedroom, where both of them were lying in one bed, head to foot. Just then, their father joined me.

"Hon, we have to take them to the hospital. They're getting worse," he said, his voice heavy with concern.

"I know, dear," I replied softly. "But please—help me trust God for their healing. If they're not better by morning, we'll take them to the hospital."

Though I spoke with calm resolve, my mind was deeply troubled. Still, I was determined to learn more about divine healing and hold on to that hope.

I am not sure of exactly what my Husband's reply was; but I am sure it was in approval of my request concerning the boys.

Before that night I had never slept more soundly.

Just after sunrise, I was awakened by a rhythmic tapping, like something striking an empty tub. Curious, I stepped out of my room to investigate—and there they were: Ellio and Kimbert, sitting happily in the middle of the living room, beating one of my kitchen pans with wooden spoons, alive with energy and laughter.

I woke their dad and pointed to the boys. "Do they have fever?" he asked. I admonished him to go and check on them and see, "They do not have -they are cool!"

Yes -God healed both of our boys from that Virus.

Experienced and written by: Corine V. Solomon

"An Eye Infection"

My husband, two youngest sons and I had moved into our new home in Crew Road for just about a year when I started having some problem in my left eye, sometime it felt like my eye was being stuck with small needles other times I could not turn them to either side or rub them, I used all the home remedies that I knew or heard of – but still the agony with my eyes grew worse this I endured for three or four days.

Our sons went off to school, and my husband left for work. Like every other day, I cherished my quiet time alone—devotion, even if it was no more than a simple prayer.

Feeling the pain in my eye I decided to see how my eye looked - so I went to one of the long mirrors that separates my bathroom and clothes closet, on turning the light on, I took a closeup view of my eye by using my fingers to expose the ball, I noticed a discoloring and then a small yellow warm like thing coming out of the lower part of my left eye.

Though in pain, I cleaned and washed my eyes, asking God to please help me.

Having already managed to fix the family lunch and served my husband his.

After he had gone, I decided to place a wet cloth over my eyes and rest a while. in fixing to rest, I covered a section of my already dressed bed with an extra sheet, and rested myself in a cape-in-corner position, which has always been my habit when I rested in the day.

I was only resting for a short time when I felt that I was not alone -this was a feeling I had by that time became familiar with.

I hadn't been lying down long, just beginning to drift into a nap, when I suddenly felt a powerful presence in my bedroom. It was located at the foot of my bed and brought with it a deep, calming peace that filled the entire room. Curious and slightly awed, I tried to turn my head to see what it was—but quickly realized I couldn't move any part of my body. Still eager to look, I attempted to shift my eyes, but becaúse of my eye condition, their movement was limited. Even so, I managed to catch a glimpse—a tall figure clothed in what seemed to be a familiar shade of blue. I wouldn't say I saw it on my own; rather, I believe I was allowed to see it.

Along with that brief vision came a voice, one I instinctively recognized as my grandmother's—my mother's mother. The voice gently instructed: *"Squeeze a few drops of lime juice into a cup of cool, boiled water, and use it to wash your eyes."*

The strong presents at the foot of my bed then debated, it had not very long lightened up when I was able to move -after thinking a-bit of what had just taken place; I got up and went to my kitchen being well aware that I was not alone -as I am almost at all times, Pouring the boiled water from my kettle into a small bold covered it with my dish towel -I took a lime from my fridge washed it and cut it and in my effort to squeeze it I pondered "how much of the juice should I put." When I heard what I thought to be a strong mind: "squeeze till you can just taste the Juice.' I began to squeeze timidly and soon heard: "That is enough." I stopped, and tasted the water, and to me it was just right.

Well -I never took my planned nap that day, I washed my eyes with the lime water, which stung them a bit, but soon brought a cooling to them.

Through my inquiry mind I made ready to visit my Mother – reaching her home I found both of my parent in the kitchen and after greeting them and sharing a little concerning my eye problem -I asked my mother if she recalled anything her Mother used if she had any eye problem, she told me of how Grand-ma would use by sprinkling of Bazil seeds in her eyes -these she shared that Grand-ma used to collect mucus from her eyes, then she added: but for any other eye problem she would use lime Juice in cool boiled water.

I then shared with my parent what had taken place at my home.

The Lime water eye wash -I used for three days, and my eyes were as good as ever.

It is a bit in that vision that I still question a bit, well -maybe one day -my question will be answered.

Experienced and written by: Corine V. Solomon

"A Bible Study"

I grew up in Grand Cayman from the young age of six years the majority of my family and I residence while I was a child was in the vicinity of West bay, having married at a young age I have resided in George town for many years, these moves enable me to become fairly acquainted with a fair amount of the island people, within the group of people I became fairly acquainted with were an elder man who was very religious, and after many years he built a place of worship separately from where he grew up worshiping in.

One day, while I was at the government hospital, I received a call on my cell phone from an unfamiliar number. To my surprise, it was the same man I had mentioned earlier. By now, he had become a pastor in the very tabernacle he had built.

In this call he asked me to meet him at his church, feeling a little odd as always when I hear people say: My Church -but I hid my feeling and made no comments on the issue – but I informed him that I would be willing to meet him after my appointment, but I would first have to go home and ask my husband to accompany me, he then informed me that there was a female cleaner working there -so I agreed to meet him and listened to what he wanted.

I reached his Tabernacle just after two in the afternoon.

Because the cleaner was working in his office at the time, we sat together in the auditorium. There, he shared a story with me about two young people who had come from another church to visit his. They had asked him if he would marry them—but with one specific question: would he be willing to perform the ceremony *with* the exchange of wedding rings?

Long before he reached the point of the wedding rings -I was pondering on: why was this man sharing this with me? at the end of his statement, he inquired of me what he should do, so I asked him what was his conviction on the wearing of the wedding rings and he with a lengthy explanation finally confessed to me that he did not believe that God was pleased with the wearing of rings or any kind of jewelry, so I told him: that if I was in your place I would stand on my conviction.

He then said: But if I do not marry them with the ring, they will not come back to church.

I then admonished him that if they truly wanted to marry with rings they would had stayed where they were, and I tried to show him that the young people was seeking truth, and went on to tell him a story that had taken place in my home a few years earlier which was: One of my teen age sons began sneaking girls into his bedroom late at night while we slept - well this is a very long story as I acquainted his father of my findings and asked three time that he speak to our son concerning his disrespectful actions in our home reminding him that we had dedicated our home to The Lord.

Well, the ball had returned to my court, so I confronted our son. I reminded him of the choices he was making—how they were affecting his soul—and the consequences that could follow. I told him firmly that he could no longer use our home to support a sinful lifestyle. If he chose to continue, he would need to find a place of his own.

And so, our son left. He stayed away from us for two years.

The day he finally came to visit, he asked me, "Mama, did you think I wasn't coming back to the house?" Then, looking me in the eye, he added, "I want to tell you—if you hadn't handled things with me the way you did, I would have questioned your Christianity."

About a year later my husband and I accepted that Pastor invitation to a series of meeting, it was sometime in those visits he asked me if I could recall the tale concerning the couple that wanted him to marry them with wedding rings, I confessed that I did, and he told me that he married them with the rings, and after the wedding they never returned.

A few years after that, he asked me if I would host a Bible study for him. I told him I would first have to seek God's will of which I did.

I saw this only as an open door to share a bit more of the Gospel of Christ was the way I understand it, but God was allowing this move in my life because He wanted to show me something new.

I touched base with the Pastor, and arranged that I would be willing to commence the Bible study the following week, and also inquired of him the duration of time I would have to host the Bible study, and surprising me he said: that a half hour would be enough time I debated that, and he extended it to an Hour – I held the one hour Bible study once a week twice, and in my time of studying for the third lesson I was admonished in my spirit to place the props that I was planning to use in my hand bag -why was I to do that at that time; I knew not the reason -but I did as I was admonished.

All the preparations for worship before the Bible study had been completed, and not long after the study began, the pastor interrupted the lesson to answer a loud phone call on his cell. I didn't respond to it, choosing to stay focused. I was just about to begin the part of the study that involved using the props I had brought in my handbag, when once again, he interrupted—this time with words that were deeply disrespectful. Out of respect for others, I won't repeat what was said or name anyone in particular, but his words brought an abrupt and unfortunate end to the unfinished Bible study.

Of course, I was aware by then that his doctrine and the doctrine of Christ—the one I teach—were in clear conflict.

Questions for thought:

In your opinion, what do you think was his reason for requesting for me to host the Bible study?

What do you think was his main reason for crashing the Bible Study?

What exactly was God's reason for allowing me to have that experience?

What do you think I learned or should have learned from that experience?

Please, if you wish, feel free to email me your answers, if doing so, share with me where you live, and your name.

Experience and written by: Corine V. Solomon

"But I asked you Father"

Sometime in 1994 a friend of mine told me that she and her little daughter was going to Honduras, and invited me to take the trip with them.

I told her that I would have to ask my husband and father God's approval -I was almost sure that my husband would approve of me going, but what was more important to me was God's approval -therefore I took the desire of this trip to God in Sincere Prayer for weeks, I asked God: if it was not His will for me to go, then let all my efforts to prepare come to nothing—and I promised Him that I would say "Amen" and accept it. But if it was His will for me to go—or even if it was not—I asked Him to do whatever He saw fit, but to please make His will clear to me.

Well -I went about doing what I had to do to make ready, and never did I ever have one nick of disappointment with my making ready.

The day of the trip came and we were on our way boarding the thirty-five Passenger seater Plain.

I waited my turn to climb up the four step ladder that was suspended from the door of the plain by Large Rope-arms on boat sides, as only one person at a time was permitted, and a big woman was taking her time trying to enter the plain, with my plan to start climbing the steps. I rested my right hand on the top suspending Rope, and as my fingers circled the Rope, I heard a gentle whisper which said: "Bind every evil spirit on this Plain." Thank God I called on Christ Jesus for help, and in His Holy name I bound every evil spirit on the plain as I was told.

The Plain was fully loaded, the weather was great, we were nearing the end of the trip -the Plain made a slight descend for landing, and leveled off once more when I noticed that the plain beginning to circle when this was done two or three times I got out of my seat and went over to my friend telling her in a whisper to Pray with me as something was wrong with the plain, On my second trip I asked her to join me in Prayer, she took a small bottle of Oil from her hand bag.

As I returned to my seat for the second time, I settled into deeper prayer. In that moment of stillness, I was made aware—within my spirit—that the plane's wheels were stuck. I shared this with my friend, then re-engaged in prayer. I reminded God, "Father, I had asked You if it was Your will for me to come on this trip…"

Then, deep within, I was gently questioned: *"If this would save one soul, are you willing to go through this?"*

I paused and thought about it for a few seconds. Then I answered, with full sincerity, "Yes, Father." For truly, seeing souls saved is one of my greatest desires.

By this time, I noticed that the Plain was still circling, the people was all still all busy chatting, I saw that high twilight of the evening as I looked out the window, wishing to see how high the Plain was I noticed that below us were different size boats, and flying close beside us were a few other Plains, and as far as my memory solves, I think I heard the sound of a helicopter.

It was not until then that I noticed that some of the passengers behind me were beginning to peep through the windows, and that others were becoming stirred.

I once again resumed in quiet Prayer and there in -my indignation rose, and with my folded hands I tapped hard against the seat in-front of me, and just then it seemed as if a car had fallen out of the plain, and I felt assured that the wheels of the Plain were released.

Let me here say: that I am in no way implying that it was my hands that brought down the wheels of the Plain but the Mercy of God through the sincere Prayers that had touched God's heart.

As we landed, the pilot—or perhaps the co-pilot, I wasn't sure—headed toward the door. My friend stopped him and asked in Spanish, "What was the problem with the plane?"

He replied, "Nothing—it was just that the airport was congested with traffic."

I am not fluent in Spanish but God blessed me in understanding what they had said, and having been by that time making my way to move out of my seat, I reached across and tugged him by his right back Pocket, and told him that he was telling a lie. He just turned around, glanced at me, and continued to the door, which he opened.

Minutes after that we had landed safely on La Ceiba airport, which was filled with Police cars, ambulances, and I would guess that there were as much People outside the Airport Terminal as there was inside.

I continued in quiet prayer giving God thanks for His Blessing towards all of us.

I often wonder if there was either soul from that flight awakened to their condition and surrendered to God -even now I hope that there was at least some one that was at the airport that surrendered to God.

Well—I don't know, but praise God, He does. And if there was any, and we remain faithful, one day we will meet in heaven.

Experienced and written by: Corine V. Solomon

"Called a Witch"

It was a weekday, and I was home alone as my husband was at work and my two youngest sons were in school.

It was almost mid evening when the Phone rang for the very first time that day, I answered it and learned that it was the female pastor from the congregation we attended that was on the line, I identified myself and told her to hold on for a minute -I took the Phone out of its charging stand and went to my bedroom to rest and chat, if that would by chance be.

The Pastor told me that she called me to tell me that she wanted me to go to pray for a sister that was sick now for many a week, she went on to informed me that the sister mother had taken her to all the Doctors on Island and in the United States that she could afford, and that they the elders of the church had all prayed for her healing, but she is still sick.

"Pastor, are you asking me to go and pray for her? Remember: I am Corine, the one that all of you in the congregation well except one, have always rejected."

There was a bit of a pause on the other end of the line -then the Pastor said: "Sister Corine, if I have offended you, please forgive me."

"If! -are you using it as a badge of doubt or as a conjunction?" I questioned her.

"I'll pray about visiting the sister; if it is God's will that I go -I will."

It was quickly made clear to me that God had laid it on the pastor's soul to ask me to go pray for the young sister, but I, from the day she called me, always wondered if she ever knew exactly what God was saying to her.

If I told this story in total, it would be quite lengthy, but herein I am only sharing just enough to glorify God's name.

I left my home after lunch the next day to go visit my young sister, I reached her home at one-fifty-five.

I told her that I had only just learned yesterday that she was unwell, and I let her know that if there was anything I could do to help, she should tell me—and I would do my best to assist her.

Without telling her the story of how visiting her came about - I read three out of the four scriptures inthat had been impressed upon my heart the day before to share with her. I paused for a moment before attempting to read the fourth, as God knew I needed Him to give me more courage to do everything I was sent to do. Though it may seemed simple, but to me that day, it felt like climbing a mountain—and God knew exactly why.

James 5: 14-16, I announced and went on to read the fourth scripture. I then asked her if she wished me to pray for her -after all, that was what I was sent there to do.

"I can't allow you to pray for me," she said; as she slipped almost to the edge of her bed and went on to tell me that they all know that I was a witch, just then I was admonished and strengthen in my soul to kneel beside her bed as she proceeded to inform me of acts of which they knew I had done, I was shocked to hear all what she said. They—which I understood to be a group—had ostracized me, but I wasn't shocked to learn this.

When she was finished her uncontrollable talking, I was able to arise from the side of her bed and advised her that I was leaving, and as I placed my hand on the door knob, she said: "Sister Corine; would you Pray for me?" I returned to her bed, told her a funny but true story about anointing oil, which caused her to smile, and Praise God I was granted clearance to anoint and pray for her.

I was told by her helper the next day that surprisingly she arose well and Hearty and went to her Job of which she had not been able to attend to for some weeks - I don't recall how many weeks passed during which the helper told me that her mistress was off work, but I thank and praise God for rescuing her and for answering my prayer to understand the reason behind the rejection.

I thank God that I know that He has never begun a job that He will not finish -and this one, thus far though unfinished will be no less, for as I have said He have never started any job He have not finished, but there is a time for everything.

All the Thanks, praise, glory, and honor belongs to God Almighty.

Experienced and written by: Corine V. Solomon

"Dislocated Foot"

A few years after I was sanctified I sat in the tabernacle awaiting the Worship service to commence -the Pastor of that time, his wife, and their youngest son -who I assumed was twelve or thirteen years old entered The moment I saw him, it was strongly impressed upon my heart to tell his parent to strap his foot. I recall it as being his left foot any way – the message was that they were to band his entire heel to his leg in a very firm manner anoint him and Pray for his healing as the problem he was having with his foot was very serious.

I knew that I had to deliver this message, but I was hesitant in speaking of it in the service as I knew from then that all things are not free to reveal, so I held my peace and I went to their house the next day -his mother was at home, I was again hesitant to speak to her, but God blessed me with the strength to do so.

After delivering the message to her -she told me that they had taken their son to a doctor years before and they were told that he had a spur heal, and that he would outgrow it, I must add: she seemed to be willing to hold on to the diagnose of the doctor, which made me feel at that time a bit defeated, but what I later learned or was reminded of: God is never wrong.

Despite my feeling of defeat, or rather another act of rejection, I admonished her to take heed and attend to his foot.

I wish to pause here and once again give God thanks and all the glory for His love and mercy towards us, His unworthy creation.

Some weeks later, I met with her again, and she told me that on the very evening of the day I had visited her home and mentioned her son's foot, he came home from school in severe pain and discomfort. It was so serious that she had to rush him to a private doctor. After examining his foot, the doctor immediately ordered an X-ray of his leg and foot. Upon reviewing the results, he told her that she needed to take her son to a specialized hospital in Miami as soon as she could catch a flight—the issue was that his foot was not fully connected to his leg, and it was something that could not be treated on the island. Praise God, the young man was attended to and was successful and is yet alive and well.

I thank God for His faithfulness and Grace unto even those that choose to walk life their way, but yet I pray that God will save that young man's soul.

Experienced and written by: Corine V. Solomon

"A great Nudged by the Spirit"

My husband and I once again went to La Ceiba, Honduras to have a medical check. We resided in the home of a man we were acquainted with from the bay islands. in this home the man's niece worked for him and lived in the home.

On this trip, the man was away, and his niece showed through her actions that she appreciated our presence. She even joined us for morning devotions and Bible study, and she seemed to truly enjoy it. On the compound of the two-story house where we were staying, there was a long apartment building that stretched across the entire length of the property. The first floor of the main building were also used as a rented apartment, where a man lived his wife and young child.

The second night we were there, I was greatly troubled in my spirit in such a way that I was unable to sleep all night, but thank God, I made it a night of sincere and intercessory Prayer -this great Nudging in my spirit was an admonishment to leave this house.

In the early hours of the morning when my husband woke, I told him that I wished to leave that morning and go to a hotel for the balance of our stay, but withheld my deep reason with the intention of sharing it with him after we were settled in the hotel.

At breakfast I shared with the young woman -that we would be moving over to the Iberia Hotel for the rest of our vacation. I sensed that she was quite upset by the news, but I extended an invitation for her to join us at the hotel for our Bible study and Sunday worship, as we would not be attending any of the local congregations.

After checking into the hotel, I called her to inform of our room number, and it was then that I learned that she was somewhat offended by our leaving the house, but I then encouraged her to come over on Sunday, and I would explain our action to her.

The young woman joined us for devotion and a short Bible study in our hotel room, and it was after our little worship that I told her and my husband the reason why I had to leave the house, after which she shared the shooting up that took place on the compound the late night of Friday -I thanked and Praised God for enabling and accepting my Intercessory Prayer for the people on that compound.

The reason why father did not want us to remain on that compound was because he did not wish us to experience the shooting out, if there were any other reason why -he did not reveal it to us.

The story of what caused the shooting -I feel it cannot bring any glory to God is the reason why I have not shared it.

Experienced and written by: Corine V. Solomon

"Fornication Exposed"

It was early on a Saturday morning when someone knocked on my front door. Standing just outside the entrance arch of my porch were a young woman and two young men.

After questioning the reason for their call -the young woman took up the role of spoke person, inquiring of rent vacancy, she went on to explain that they were strangers and were very much in need of a dwelling place as they had to leave where they were residing due to the owner having to do renovation to the building.

I inquired from her how many persons that she was seeking rent for, two, she replied, which two? I asked. My husband and I, she replied.

Just then, deep in my soul, I heard: "Fornication."

I informed her that she would have to give me a legal marriage certificate, as I do not rent to unmarried couples. she then told me that they did not travel with it, but that she would send to her country, requesting for it.

I was in belief that they were not married, and I did what I could to discourage renting her.

Sunday morning, as my husband and I were driving on our way out to attend Sunday school, still on the private road beside our home, the young woman waved us down wanting to pay half of the rent and security deposit.

I took it from her informing her that If I was assured that they were not married I would be giving them seventy-two hours eviction notice, which I had to do about two weeks later, as it was proven to me that the man was a married man from Jamaica, but first I had to repent to God for not heeding to His voice, it is wise that all God's children learn His voice; and obey His leading.

I thank and praise Father God for the many times He has and will allow His permissive will in my life, and I am without words to express but glad to know that whatever is in His fix will it will surly come to pass.

I thank Father God for the grace He bestows upon us each day as we walk the narrow path that leads to eternal life—a journey in which we learn to die to self, that we may truly live.

Experienced and written by: Corine V. Solomon

"Hurricane Warning"

One day in early September 2004, I felt a solemn prompting in my spirit to take my anointing oil and anoint my home, along with all the other buildings on our property. I faithfully carried out this act, and just a few days later—on what I now distinctly remember as the eighth day of September that very year—something significant unfolded. Before that morning, I was in devotion in my Bay window, my favorite spot for devotion, writing, or just resting.

After my private prayer time that morning had ended, I remained seated in my recliner chair. In the stillness, I heard a whisper—as if spoken directly into my ear—saying, "Category Five, Category Five." I cannot presently recall whether I had prayed about this specific matter earlier that morning.

On mingling with the members of my family that morning -when coming in touch with my fourth son, he said to me: "Mama there is a Category three Hurricane heading our way, and I plan to leave the Island going into Honduras with my wife and baby and I would like if you and dad go with us." I replied to him: "Bo, it will not be a Category three, it will be a Category five." "No ma'am it is a Category three." He replied. I once again repeated that it will be a Category five, and added, well is it safe to go there? The Hurricane can also go there, I believe he thought soundly on my maybe speech, anyway it was not long when he returned sharing his desire for his dad and I to go to Honduras with them, as he knew if he could persuade me to go, his dad would follow.

I took my son's heartfelt plea for us to join them on the trip to Honduras to God in sincere prayer. My concern over this matter deepened, as I knew that if I chose to go, I would also need to take my mother with me.

When reaching the Hotel in La Ceiba, I went Prostrate on the floor before God begging Him for mercy on the people and the Island.

On returning to the Island which was a bit difficult to recognize due to the damages from the Hurricane.

Thank and Praise to His Holy name our Home and family was taking care of along with so many others.

And as always: God was once again merciful and faithful to us all.

Experienced and written by: Corine V. Solomon

"My Mother-in-law's Choice"

My Mother-in-law fell seriously sick in the year of 2004 and was hospitalized.

She had been in the hospital for three days before we were able to visit her. Upon entering her room, we saw that her second-youngest child—a devoted daughter—was there by her side. The nurses informed us that she was recovering well.

Two days later we were notified that she was not doing very well. My husband was at work, so I told my mother who lived next to me that I was going to the hospital to visit and Pray for my Mother-in-law, and mother requested that I wait for her to get ready as she wished to go along to visit her.

Reaching the room we saw that her faithful daughter was again with her, and that she was lying face to the wall we called to my mother-in-law but received no respond, from her -my mother then reach over in the front of her and took a hold of her left arm, and in reinstating her arm mother signaled me that she was low -I then told mother and my sister-in Law that I was going to have Prayer for her, requesting that we hold hands I was able to rest my left hand on her left hip at the ending of the short Prayer a nurse entered the room, as to give the nurse room to do her duty we left the small room which was already crowded with the tree of them.

The next day, around lunchtime, I returned to visit her. As I entered the room, I saw the same nurse who had been there the evening before, along with my sister-in-law. My mother-in-law was sitting up in a chair with a table in front of her, eating her lunch.

I expressed great joy at seeing her sitting up and eating, clearly stronger than before. Then the nurse turned to me and said, "Madam, I assume you are a Christian, because God heard your prayer for your mother-in-law—she was a dying woman just yesterday.

I Praised God openly; and visited a bit longer before leaving the hospital with rejoicing and thanksgiving in my heart. I made my way home.

The following day my mother-in-law was discharged from hospital to reside with us until she was fully able to return to her home.

In the early morning, the next day I was admonished in my spirit to give my husband a message concerning his mother.

When he was up, ready for work, before he left our home, I shared the message with him.

Before delivering the message to him, I shared with him my experience in receiving of the message of which I was about to give him.

"Timothy, two of your family members will come here to collect your mother, and she will be willing to go with them to their home, from where in a short time she will be taken into hospital where she will pass on."

On Timothy's way to the door in an effort to leave for work, two of his family members came, stating that they were here to collect his mother.

Timothy invited them inside, and in their presence, he asked his mother if she wished to stay with them or stay with us -she said that she wanted to go with them, holding up his right hand with his fingers separated Timothy asked her to look at him and on she doing so, he asked her how many fingers did she see, and she replied: "I see five fingers Tim."

He then repeated his first question to her, and she once more gave him the same reply.

Ok, Mom, you have made your choice.

Three days after my mother-in-law left our home, she was placed in the hospital, and three days later in the hospital she passed away.

Though saddened by her death of which I will probably always believe was untimely.

I give God thanks for His faithfulness towards us in that season as always, but-especially towards Timothy even in helping him to be prepared for his mother's passing.

Experienced and written by: Corine V. Solomon

"Gifts for the Children"

Since the early 1970s, I began a donation ministry to help anyone in need, though my primary focus was on underprivileged children. My most significant outreach effort was directed toward the children of Guanaja in the Bay Islands.

The only way of transport to and from there back then was by way of small ships which took passengers, cargo, and food supplies of different kind; these trips were made sometimes every two weeks or once a month.

The year 1978 was a particularly difficult one for my family, and as the holiday season approached, it was time for me to begin gathering whatever I could to send as Christmas gifts to the children in Guanaja.

I began to grow anxious, fearing that I might not be able to send even a small gift to the children that year. Troubled by this thought, I turned to prayer, earnestly asking God to help me find a way to send something—anything—for them. If memory serves me correctly, the transport vessel—which we referred to back then simply as *The Boat*—had already made its final trip for October. That meant I had only two more chances to ship whatever I could gather in time for Christmas. One mid-afternoon on a weekend in early november – I am sure that it was a weekend because all of my children were at home, sometime before lunch that day, one of the children ran in the house telling me that there were some people on the porch wishing to see me.

Opening my front door, standing there were two white males and a female who seemed to have been feeling the effects of the tropical sun, as their skin was already pink.

After our greetings they told me that they had brought the gifts for the children. - . I heard their words, but in that moment, I didn't fully grasp the depth of what they were saying or the significance of their visit. All I understood was that I was to accept the gifts and make room in the house for the many boxes I saw loaded onto the white pickup truck parked in our front yard.

The boxes were arrived in by the three visitors, with help from my two young sons. They were lined up in two neat rows, stretching down our hallway and into the family room, all the way to the side of our loveseat. When there was no more space left, I opened my bedroom to accommodate the remaining boxes.

I thanked them and in their leaving I peeped out the window of my family room in an effort to see them go, but they were not there, but even with that I was not awoken to what had taken place, how could that be?

Later that day, my son Ellio, who was nearly nine years old at the time, said to me, "Mom, those people who brought the boxes—they're not real people, they're angels." Even as I listened to him, the full weight of what had happened hadn't yet settled in. It wasn't until sometime later that I truly realized—God had answered my prayer by providing the gifts I needed to send to the children. In writing this testimony, I was saddened to think that I could have at least offered them some cool water.

Why was my understanding not given freedom of this until a later time?

Only God fully knows; and I give Him thanks for so doing because He does all things well, and now, years later, I understand a bit more about my why nots.

I thank and praise Him for all He has done for and through me and for all He will still do as He has reminded me that I can bring forth fruit in my old age.

I must add that I have a very inquirer mind, therefor despite what I had experienced from the visitors who brought the gifts for the children -I had the area where I lived investigated in effort to find out if any strangers had given gifts to any of the neighbors, the results were that no one had even seen any strangers.

Learning of this, I was satisfied and settled that once more I was granted a visit by Angels.

Experienced and written by: Corine V. Solomon

"Nineteen Eighty-six Revival in Savannah"

I made plans to attend the night services of the revival due to the responsibilities of my children, and my husband would care for them at night.

The first service commenced on Sunday, of which my family and I attended, as always -the revival services would go on until the following Sunday.

I reminded my husband on Monday before he left for work of my plan to attend the service Monday night.

Evening was drawing near, and I was rushing to get ready and head out, determined not to be late for the start of the service. But I was disappointed when I started my car—only to realize it was low on gas. Yes, I had completely forgotten all day to fill the tank. Noticing my disappointment, I called my husband's attention to the situation. He took a piece of hose and a gallon bottle, then siphoned two gallons of gas from his truck and poured it into my car. "It's not much," he said reassuringly, "but with what's already in your tank and these two gallons, you'll make it to Savannah and back with ease.

I began my journey, carefully staying within the speed limit. But after driving for some time—how long exactly, or where I was at that moment, I cannot now recall—I realized I was suddenly speeding. I had no control over the gas pedal or the brakes. I believe I had been on the road for about half an hour or more since leaving my home, which at the time was located in North George Town.

I heard a voice repeatedly whispering "She's coming." At that time I was brought to the realization of where I was and that I had no control of my car -I was at a far distance in the east end of the Island, and at the same time I also realized that I was not alone in my car, it was then that I was reminded to pray -a few seconds after I began to call on God for help I sensed a struggling taking place in the car, and soon I felt as if something like a limb of a big coconut tree covered me from my left shoulder and extended all the way over to the front passenger seat instantly thereafter I felt that I was able to get control of my car, and as if by a street light I saw a flat ground and was admonished deep in my mind to reverse there and turn around.

Thank God I was able to turn around and head back to town -not very long after I was on the way back; the whispering which I heard only twice changed into: "She's going."

By that time I had grown almost calm and comfortable, fully aware that God was taking care of me. As I looked ahead, I saw three women in the distance who appeared to be well up in age, dressed like saints. One was walking close to the left side of the road, gently leading a bicycle. Another walked on the right side of the bicycle, and the third—who was the tallest of the three—followed behind them, holding an open umbrella.

On seeing them I was greatly urged to stop and pick them up -after all they were elder woman, and probable had far to walk, but a strong admonishment engulfed my mind instructing me not to do so, and praise God I was aided in driving by them, but yet another problem arose: I saw steam coming from the seam in the hood of my car, and was once again attacked this time with the fair, that my car was over heating and would catch on fire if I did not stop, than I recalled what little gas had been put in the car -looking at the gas gauge I saw that there was only one line on the gauge.

Believing that if I did not stop at the nearest gas station the car would run dry, and I would not get home -again I began to ask God for help and was quickly admonished to keep on driving, and once more I was able to follow that lead that made the difference in my Soul, and shortly I began to wonder what exactly had taking place why I had driven so far and so fast.

As I reached the area nearing the tabernacle in Savannah still in ponder over the ordeal that had taken place -I was mocked in my mind with the words: "You did not know where you were going, you are stupid." Those words seemed to be pressed deep into my mind till it seemed that they were beginning to be burned into my soul.

As I neared the church building—about fifty feet away—I switched on my left indicator. Upon reaching the gate, beside the Poinciana tree in the yard, I turned in, parked, locked my car, and quietly entered the ongoing service, which continued for just about twenty more minutes before closing. Entering the building, I saw a vacant space in the very last bench on the right side where a sister of mine was sitting, as I sat beside her, she looked at me and said: "You are late; the service is almost over, and your blouse is ripped." In a low voice, I tried to explain, but she hushed me up, and said: "You did not know where you were going."

I replied to her: "That is just what the devil tried telling me."

Dear reader I do not know what you will think or say that this experience of mind was, but as for me I believe and have closed it off as Just another Lesson for me to see that God protects His people, and also for some other to see that the enemy of the Soul which are covered by the Blood of Christ Jesus can't be destroyed because of the one in whom they serve, and I am now reminded of the comforting words in Isiah 54: 17.

My sister and Brother, I admonish you to stand fast in the Lord, and no weapon that is formed against you will prosper. this does not mean that we will not be attacked, but that the plan of the enemy will not be successful.

I am here reminded that all thing works together for the good of those that love the Lord. Romans 8 28.

Experienced and written by: Corine V. Solomon

"Attacked in Broad Daylight"

I had been working around the house since early morning, as I did almost every day. My husband had come home for lunch and returned to work, and the children had not yet arrived from school. It was—if I recall correctly—a little after two o'clock. The day was hot, I was tired, and a dull ache had settled in my back and in the calves of my legs. Knowing the relief I often found by stretching out on the floor, I went to my room, tossed a pillow down, and lay on the floor.

First, I pulled my legs up to bring my back into full contact with the floor, and soon after, I felt a welcome release from the aching. Finding comfort in that, I turned onto my left side, tucked my legs into a relaxed position, and within just a few quiet minutes, something strange and terrifying began to happen.

Though I was not asleep—not even drifting—I became acutely aware that my body was being attacked. I felt as though some large, forceful object was trying to enter me. Wide awake and fully alert, just as I am now, I reached over with my right hand and grasped the object. In that instant, I sensed the presence of its bearer.

But just as quickly, I became aware of another presence—someone I had known since childhood as my "invisible friend"—whom I later understood to be my guardian angel. With all the strength I had, I began to call on God, crying out for help as I struggled with all my might to resist this spiritual assault. I clung to the object, refusing to let it succeed in its purpose.

Thanks be to God; the struggle was short. The object suddenly vanished from my grip, and its bearer departed from the room. The spiritual war had ended, and God's protection had prevailed once again.

After supper that evening I told my husband my adventure of the day, while sharing this with him, I felt some resentfulness from him, and I said to him: I perceive that you do not believe that such a thing could happen. He did not reply to me which reconfirmed my perception, on ending my speech to him I told him that he would understand.

Did he believe that I was telling a lie? I would never believe that he did -of which I learned the truth the next early morning.

I had not long been up and was getting ready for the day, leaving him still asleep. As I made my way out of the room toward the kitchen, I noticed he was waking up with some difficulty. Sitting on the edge of the bed "Corine," he said, I was awoken by the same thing of which you were telling me that had attacked you on the floor yesterday.

Thank God, it pays to be covered by the Blood of Christ Jesus.

Experienced and written by: Corine V. Solomon

"An Old Galleon"

I attended the worship service alone this Sunday knowing that I needed to be away from my family for just a while, as it seemed that life was at that time throwing far too much at me through some of them -and being determine to fight the good fight, I desired to see if God had anything to say to me by way of the up-coming midday message concerning what was going on in my life.

I am deeply grateful that we can worship God in spirit and in truth, without always having to engage our physical bodies—because if that were not the case, my worship might not have been accepted, as my mind was overwhelmed by the many troubles that consumed my life. I sat in the pew crying my heart out without visible tears pleading with God for help. Not just to be delivered from the burdens of life, but to be set free from the tormenting accusations of the enemy of our souls, who was trying to crush my spirit with lies: that I was facing all these problems because God had rejected me, because I had failed Him

Being reassured that I was still settled in the Lord was my priority, and that I asked of Him.

I was conscious that the Service was proceeding after the opening Prayer and God knows I tried off and on to engage in the singing part of the worship, which was over after the singing of three or four songs just before the very last song was finish: I was given a Vision; in which I saw that the Tabernacle from the Pulpit down were blue Ocean Water upon which was an Old Galleon Ship smoothly sailing and I was aware that I was onboard.

The vision ceased as calmly as it had appeared. Then, a deep joy flooded my soul, and I was assured that all would be well—that even this problem, too, would pass.

In that moment, and ever since, I have come to know that it is best for every one of the Father's children to surrender completely to Him We are assured in the Holy Word in many of its books of Father's keeping, but one Scripture stands out very clearly in my mind now, and that is Isaiah 54 17.

Experienced and written by: Corine V. Solomon

"A Big Frog"

After over twenty years of worshiping at the same branch of the congregation where I was first saved, I became discouraged. Though I had a deep zeal to serve the Lord, repeated rejection of my efforts left me feeling disheartened. I struggled to worship God sincerely with the little I was allowed to do. Then, one day, I was invited by one of my daughters-in-law's to visit the congregation she attended. I accepted, and before long, I was asked to work with their teens—a task I gladly took on during their Friday night gatherings.

Of course, I had none other teaching to offer the teens but the Gospel of Christ. My time working with them lasted, all told, about three and a half months. During that period, as I continued attending this place of worship, I began to notice that it lacked certain elements I believe should be present in any place where God is worshiped. I shared my concerns with the pastor, and to my surprise, I was given full permission to do whatever I felt necessary to improve the appearance of the sanctuary.

The first Saturday after I my conversation with the pastor, I went to Town and purchased some artificial flowers enough to create two Vase arrangements, which I planned to place one on each side of the rostrum.

While driving back from town, I remembered that I had the key to the front door of the worship hall, so I decided to stop by and drop off the flowers. Upon reaching the front door, I realized it was unsafe. As I stepped into the middle of the small auditorium, I heard voices—though not clearly. I wasn't surprised, as I had learned that Saturdays were the usual day for cleaning and preparing the space for Sunday services

I placed the flowers inside the Communion table and was urged to go make my presence known to the others that was there.

As I approached the door from which the muffled voices were coming, I saw it was slightly ajar. I gave a gentle knock and was invited in by the pastor's mother—known to the congregation as the Mother of the Church. As I stepped inside, I noticed all the girls from the youth meeting gathered around a table. My eyes shifted toward the woman, and in that very moment, I saw something astonishing—a large frog emerged from her left shoulder, just above her chest. It leaped across the room and landed on the window, which was about eight or nine feet away from where she sat at the end of the table. Then, just as suddenly as it had appeared, it vanished.

I being well acquainted with that room just as I was with all the others in that building, I knew that it was impossible for that big Frog to just varnish, I think it was on this thought that I first realized that I was being shewn who that woman was.

Some days after that I learned from one of the girls who attended the Friday night youth meeting -that the woman had secretly summonsed the them to meet her there that evening, and that she questioned them about what I was teaching them, and of course coached them with whatever she did.

A few days after the incident, a meeting was held at the place of worship. At the close of the meeting, the pastor's mother announced that they would be hosting a gathering at the hall on the night of the upcoming Halloween. The purpose, she explained, was to offer the children an alternative, shielding them from the negative influences associated with Halloween activities. She mentioned that costumes would be allowed, but firmly warned that no one was to dress as a witch. She then instructed the person who was listing the evening's activities to place her name last on the program.

I was present at the gathering held on the 31st of October. When that woman came forward to present her act, I must say—I believe many who had attended the earlier meeting where she first announced the plan were quite surprised by what they saw. But God knows, I was not. Though she had strictly warned others not to dress as a witch, there she was—dressed from head to toe like one, seated at a table with a crystal ball. I must admit, I felt a bit embarrassed. And why was I embarrassed? I suppose it was because she was professing to be a child of God.

Any way after the gathering was over, I was in the kitchen helping to clean up, when the woman walked into the Kitchen, handed me a well loaded white envelope and announced the contents of the letter, evidently just to allow the others in the Kitchen and all that was capable of hearing know that the family of them had written me out of their Church.

The essence of that letter was to let me know that the Post of working with the young people in their Church would no longer be needed, and the reason was that I was teaching the doctrine of Christ, this letter was signed by the Pastor, his wife, and his mother.

To this I said: thank God its nice to be thrown out of some clubs, but the seed has already been planted and will rip up the floor and tear down the walls -within a short time the congregation was partly dissolved, and within about three years I heard that the woman who was the mother of the pastor was found head down drowned in her bath tub, and the entire family left the Island.

All I can say to this is: it is a fearful thing to fall in the hands of an angry God.

No one can mock God and get by.

Experienced and written by: Corine V. Solomon

"Healed from Tumors"

In 1980, I noticed that I was having a rapid weight gain, accompanied by lack of energy, and soon after, I was not able to sleep in my favorite position -my stomach, weeks after all of the unwelcome action in my body. I often off and on felt movement, as if I were with child, but the test proved that untrue.

Dissatisfied with the medical results I received on the island, my husband took me to a hospital in Florida for a second opinion. After a thorough examination, the doctor informed us that all of my reproductive organs were filled with tumors and that I would need surgery within two weeks. We returned home immediately to make the necessary preparations for the upcoming procedure.

On the second night after returning home, I lay in bed beside my husband, who was sleeping peacefully next to me—his back resting gently against my left arm. In that quiet moment, vivid memories returned to me—memories of the many ways in which God had manifested His power in my life. I meditated on those moments for a while, and then turned to God in prayer. I told Him that I know He could do all things. I reminded Him of some of His promises, and with a sincere heart, I pleaded with

Him to heal my body from the tumors. I expressed my deep desire not to leave my children behind, and I asked Him to help me find something meaningful to say to my husband to explain why I wouldn't be returning to the doctor in Miami.

With all sincerity, I asked God to give me proof of my healing—specifically, by allowing my leg to fall asleep. I then stretched out my right arm—perhaps intending to rest it across my forehead, as I often do—but instead, my fingers touched the bedside lamp on my night table. At that exact moment, I felt a tall presence standing beside my bed. I sensed an arm being stretched over me, and just then, my husband's body suddenly flinched away from mine.

I tried to open my eyes as I desired to see who was standing beside my bed, but with all my effort I could not even move one of my fingers -and soon learned that my entire body was fully asleep, I knew not that night of any urge to sleep as I do not recall ever awakening until early morning.

Later that day, I shared with my husband what had taken place the night before. I told him that God had healed me, and because of that divine intervention, I had decided not to return for the surgery.

I do not recall him making any comments in agreement or disagreement according to what I had shared with him, but he did tell me that the time for him to visit his customers in Cayman Brac would be in a few days and that he thought it would be good for me to get a second opinion from the doctor there.

A few days thereafter my mother came to my house to visit -on reaching me who at that time was in my room resting, asked me how I was feeling and I told her I was feeling fine and testified to her that I was healed, looking down at me she said: "but child your stomach is still big." I replied: but I am healed.

In Cayman Brac, a few days later, and after the doctor examined me, he told my husband and I that all he found would pass away in the first act of nature upon me.

In spite of the second Opinion in the Brac my husband still insisted that I return to the Doctor in Miami, I agreed with him to attend the doctor, but stood my ground that I was not going under any surgery.

We were at the Hospital in Miami on the date and time as was originally appointed.

We were informed by a nurse that the doctor would first have to examine and assess me, and I would soon be called. assumed she meant before I could be admitted for surgery. The nurse, dressed in the modern uniform common these days, wore light purple pants and a blouse with a deep, dark purple background. The blouse was crowded with stamped patterns that included white—but what exactly those printed objects were, I can no longer recall.

Finally, I was called and led into an examination room which was only a bed surrounded by a thick U-shaped navy blue curtain with only one opening, which was in the north end of the foot of the bed.

The examination procedure was soon over, and the doctor told me I could get dressed and then come to him.

His desk and chair were located slightly northeast of the opening of the privacy curtain which hung about eighteen to twenty inches from the floor.

I aimed not to get up out of the bed until I made sure that he was not returning -looking in the direction he went, I noticed that he sat in the chair in front of the small desk -this was revealed to me by I seeing the legs of the furniture and almost his in tire left leg.

I was still in bed when a nurse entered the room—dressed in the traditional all-white uniform, complete with the small cap perched neatly on the back of her head and white wedge-heeled lace-up shoes. I didn't take in the full details of her attire until she was exiting the room. She had entered through the curtain at the head of the bed, a direction that, at the time, I didn't think much of. It was only later that I remembered there was only one opening in the curtain—and it wasn't in that direction.

She stopped at the bed and with a tender look she asked: Are you a Christian?" I replied: "Yes, I am; are you? She smiled and walked right on through the curtain at the foot of the bed -it was then that I noticed her shoes.

I then dressed and went to where the doctor was. He was still writing when I sat beside the table -he looked at me and rehearsed all that he had found at the first examination and made it clear that he did not understand what happened, because he then had not found anything wrong with me.

I was able to then tell him that I was healed by God.

Three questions remain: Who was the nurse in white? What was the real reason for me to return to the Doctor in Miami? Did this experience have any spiritual effect on the Doctor?

Experience and written by: Corine V. Solomon

"A Black Fist"

Casta, the wife of one of my first cousins, met me in La Ceiba, where we spent the night at a hotel in town. We were scheduled to leave at five the next morning for a four-hour bus journey to Olanchito, her parents' hometown—a place I had long desired to visit ever since I first met her a few years earlier. The bus left the station at five thirty in the morning, not being an express The bus made numerous stops as people got on and off, and at each stop, peddlers—mostly children—sold various items outside the bus and occasionally inside.

As far as I recall, we reached the Bus station in Olanchito sometime after eleven O'clock.

We had not gone very far on the path past the bus stop on our way to her parents' house when we noticed a man sitting outside in a yard. As we continued on, I could not help but think that he was her father, so I pointed at him and asked, "Is that your father?" Since I spoke no Spanish and she did not speak English well, she answered in broken English: "Yes, that is my Papa Corina. How did you know?"

Catching sight of her, he left the yard to greet us.

After all the greetings were over and we had finished lunch, an aunt of hers—who had arrived a bit late to welcome her—came by. They decided to head to an unfinished house in the yard near her parents' home for their midday chat and siesta. Casta invited me along and made sure I joined them.

As we crossed the outdoor kitchen beside the main house, I noticed a cross made from small tree branches hanging on the entrance frame. It caught my curiosity—I wondered about its purpose. However, I didn't ask, as I had already gathered that they were Catholics.

Reaching inside the unfinished house, I saw that a room which I assumed would be the dining and family room had wooden windows and doors, and there were two small beds that were dressed.

Casta pointed to the bed against the wall that separated the room from the Kitchen, letting me know that I could rest there.

She and her aunt sat on the opposite bed beside the open window, quickly engaging in conversation. I lay down to rest, careful to keep my feet off the bed. I placed a pillow beneath my head, draped my right arm over my forehead, closed my eyes, and tried to follow as much of their conversation as I could.

Then, quite suddenly, from within the wall, I saw a large black fist—followed by an arm, nearly to the elbow—push through the surface as though it were nothing more than water. The sight startled me, and I flinched slightly, but I remained silent, holding my composure and reflecting on the vision.

When their conversation ended, Casta and her aunt returned to the main house, and I quietly followed.

Deeply moved by the vision and eager to share it with Casta, I waited carefully for the right moment. When the time felt right, I began by gently asking her not to share what I was about to tell her with her parents. I spoke slowly and deliberately, making sure she understood every word. I paused often, checking to see if she was following, and repeated myself when needed.

After I had finished recounting the vision, I pleaded with her once more not to speak of it to her parents. But her response—filled with what I perceived to be a mixture of surprise, concern, and conviction—took me aback. She said she could not keep it from them. It might, she explained, be the very answer they'd been seeking. For years, they had struggled to complete that house, meeting obstacle after obstacle. Perhaps, she said, this vision could finally explain why.

I felt a bit uneasy about her decision to share the vision. I wasn't as familiar with her parents as I was with her, and memories from the past lingered—times when others had misunderstood or spoken ill of me for sharing such things. Yet, despite my hesitation, a quiet peace settled over me. Something deeper within assured me that perhaps this was how it was meant to be. And so, I let go of my worry and became willing for her to speak.

She called her Parent and shared my vision with them, and they called her aunt and the rest of their family, who all returned to her parents' home they all gathered around where Casta and I were.

After a serious yet quiet conversation with her parents, Casta told me that they wished to know if I would be willing to return to the house and pray for its cleansing. I sat in deep thought for a few moments, quietly lifting my heart to God in response to their request. Almost immediately, I felt a sense of comfort and clarity—it became clear to me that this was the very reason the vision had been given. I agreed. Casta then told me that the family wished for me to lead the way back to the house, and they would follow.

As for how I felt in that moment, I'm not sure I can fully explain it. But what I do know is that it was a deeply humbling experience—one that touched me in a way words can barely express.

within that I was meant to walk through every part of it—and so I did, with the family following closely behind. I completed the walk and stopped in the kitchen, where it had first begun. There, I stopped and sat on a stool. The family gathered around me in a half-moon circle, holding hands and bowing their heads.

I then knelt at the stool to begin the prayer. As I did, I noticed that they had all quietly knelt as well. I had only just begun praying when, one by one, they each began to weep. Their tears flowed freely, as though something long-held was finally being released.

When the prayer came to an end, I learned something that deeply moved me. It was in that very house that the family had originally planned for Casta and me to spend the night—but she had refused to sleep there. So, her parents had given up their own bed for us instead.

The next day, after breakfast, before we left to return to La Ceiba, her father asked her to ask me where he could get a Bible like mine, and that she must tell me that my God would be his God.

All Praise, honor, and glory to His name!!!

I truly believe that family spiritual lives were impacted by God.

Experienced and written by: Corine V. Solomon

"Food for Thanks Giving Day"

One day in the early part of November in the early nineteen eighties, I was busy at my kitchen sink, when one of my children who was inside the house ran to me telling me that there were some people at the front door looking for me.

I hadn't given the child permission to open the door, but I dried my hands and followed them to the front entrance. Soon, my other children joined us as well.

When the door was opened, there stood three very fair-skinned individuals—what appeared to be a rather short woman in front, and two men behind her. All three seemed to be feeling the effects of the midday sun, their skin tinged with a noticeable pink glow. They stood to the right of the doorway, one behind the other, though not in perfect alignment—the tallest of the three stood at the back.

The female of the group handed me a ten-pound note and they said: "Take this and purchase food for Thanksgiving dinner, and we will be back on Thanksgiving Day for dinner." I thanked them and they left.

I folded the bill and tucked it behind the frame of the picture that hung on the left inside wall beside the door. I already knew I wouldn't be participating in the custom of the Thanksgiving dinner. As far as I could recall, the island people had only started observing the United States' Thanksgiving in recent years—and even then, it certainly wasn't a tradition celebrated across the entire island. After resuming my duties in the kitchen my second son tugged at the end of my blouse in great effort to get my attention. He shouted and said: "Mama, they were not real people -they are Angels." At first hearing of the statement from the child, I gave no real heed, although I did give some reply of which I do not fully remember exactly what it was, but I am sure it must have satisfied him for if it had not been knowing him, he would have been back.

Any way -The Thanks given day arrived, and I was not even conscious of it, but around nine that morning a woman that I had became quite acquainted with and her two children came to my back door, and on letting them in the mother said to me: "Miss Corine I to not have anything to cook for my children today, could you help me to do something?"

I went to my kitchen and selected a bit of all I had that could help to make a meal for them including that Largest Chicken I had in the freezer of my fridge -as I was taking the chicken out I recalled what the people had said concerning they coming for dinner, and I think it was at that time that I realized that they were all speaking at the same time but that I heard them as one voice.

I think it was the second day after this that I decided to encourage my eldest son in a dream of his childhood of being a detective, by instructing him to visit the nearby neighbors and ask if anyone had given them money to purchase food for the thanks given day -of course I encouraged him that the best way to find out was by talking to the Children.

After he had completed his detective work, there was no report that any of the other neighbours had received any money. It was then that I fully settled in my heart that, once again, we had been visited by angels.

I thanked God for once more blessing my family in this way, and that we could, in turn, be a blessing to others.

I was once more reminded of the words in scripture that admonish us to entertain strangers…Hebrews 13: 1-2.

Experienced and written by: Corine V. Solomon

"A Message from Hell"

A BIT OF MY DAD

For many years I worked with Dad concerning the salvation of his never-dying Soul.

I must say: I never ever saw my Dad attend a Church service, or even hold a conversation or ask a question concerning God, but as an adult I learned that he was deprived of attending any of the teaching of God, but yet despite he being a sinner he was very respectful unto God, many a time I heard him share of the many blessings that God had did for him, of all the sharing he did towards thanks giving to God the one that intrigued me most -was the one about the day at sea that he was suffering -almost all that day with a horrible back pain which paralyzed him to his bunk, and he remembered hearing Mother read from the Bible about some of the acts of Jesus he asked Jesus to please take away the pain, he said that -that said evening when his room was becoming dark, and he was unable to get up to turn on the light Jesus came into his room which was lite up by the light from Him, and He walked up to the side of his Bunk and placed His hand on his back and the pain left instantly...

THE MESSAGE TO DAD

I am one who can honestly say, I rarely dream, and can chance to say that 95% of the dreams I have had have been dreams of instruction of some kind for me or someone else.

I recall it to be in 1989 I had the following dream: I was walking a path from South to north, when I came across a small white house with a single Pyramid roof the entrance to the house was open -I walked inside there was not any partitions or windows, all the inside walls were white just as the outside walls.

Reaching the inside, I stood a distance from the entrance -when I noticed a white woman walking from the south towards me with staff in her right hand, she was dressed in white, her hair was an attractive light golden brown which rested on her shoulders, reaching me she handed me the staff and with out hearing any voice I knew that she was telling me to take, hold, and keep the staff, and that I had to leave then.

I walked out of the house staff in hand, and headed down the seemly well used narrow Path that was in front of me, on both sides of the Path was grass that looked manicured, after walking for a short distance caught sight of a man off on the left side of the path squatting down in front of a three stone fire hart which was on the grown, a frying pan was resting on the stones -I did not see any fire, but he was seemly preparing something to cook -which resembled a snake -as I got closer to him I notice that he was cutting it up cross way, and as I reached him he spoke to me and asked " do you want some of this?" this he said in a hoarse voice without turning his head.

I kept on walking and replied: "No, I do not." Still continuing the path which soon branched off into what seemed to be a Y – I then started thinking: which of the two paths must I go, and quickly my question was answered that I was to take the right Path which I soon learned was narrow just like the Path I had first started on.

I walked some distance when I heard a male Voice call a few times: "Anybody there for Carrie?" After hearing the call about three times I recalled hearing my father saying that when he was growing up everyone called him Carrie -on this memory, I began to look around to see who was calling seeing no one I replied to the call by saying: "Yes, I am his baby." Then suddenly I saw a place which was engulfed with flames of Boiling Lava coming up like gigantic flames all seemly boiling in Unison -as far as my eyes could see in every direction, and slowly a little man wearing a light Khaki suit of clothes -with what I call clear Biscuit skin color came running towards me with those flames seemly being part of him, but he was waving telling me: "Tell Carrie: don't come here this is an awful place." Now just imagine the Horror sight in those flames of what seems to be Boiling Lava People, men and women, young and old, of all sizes, and nations, bodies boiling up into those flames.

This was one part of this dream I did not understand the meaning for a long time I began to try to get to the little man, but suddenly there was an invisible wall that separating us, Thank God.

Days later, when I finally made up my mind, or rather got

the strength to deliver the message to my Dad: I first described the little man to my Parents asking them if they by any chance happened to have knew anyone like him my parent spoke almost in Unison: "that was your grandfather Culley hearing this I was even more hesitant to deliver the message, but realized all the more how important it was for me to deliver the message to my Dad after all his soul was hanging in the balance, and this message maybe the key to setting it free.

I can't explain how I felt to have to deliver that message, I thank God for giving me the strength to do so. I said: "Dad I hate to have to tell you this, but I have to." And I reiterated the Dream to my Parent.

After I was finish speaking Dad said to me: "I will not go to Hell Love." I replied: "You will if you do not repent, and receive forgiveness for your Sins."

Praise God Dad repented, but that is yet another Testimony.

Experienced and written by: Corine V. Solomon

"He is not the One for You"

In 1998, a female friend and I took a trip to La Ceiba, Spanish Honduras. We stayed in a cozy hotel room with two full beds, a TV, a desk, and a furnished bathroom. It was the perfect base for a fun and memorable getaway.

The second morning, even before devotion, we somehow became engaged in conversation concerning our husbands – it was then that she told me the story of what brought about her divorce.

Sitting at the foot of my bed, getting prepared to make my way to the bathroom in an effort to make ready for the day, I found myself listening to her talking about the man she was about to marry.

Still holding her conversation on the plan to marry her new found love she made the first move to the bathroom, she reaching midway between the foot of her bed and the bathroom door a premonition began to flood my mind concerning the man she was speaking of and as she made an effort to close the bathroom door behind her I call her attention by telling her that he was not in la Ceiba at that time, and that he was then with another woman, along with a few other things concerning the Character she was in love with -of home I had never met, when I was finish speaking she was staring at me and said "Co" which is the name she calls me –"how in the world do you know so much about him you have never met him?" and she went on to tell me that she would change him when they were married. It was there and then that I knew that I had to tell her -not to marry him as he was not the man for her, and he would bring her much harm if she did -of which I did.

And in June 2000, they were married, and sad but true she spent almost twenty years in a life of misery with him.

She and I have been and still is giving God thanks for His faithfulness towards her before that marriage, while she was in it, for his forgiveness towards her for going into it, and His mercy in helping her to get free from it.

Experienced and written by: Corine V. Solomon

"Attacked by Strokes"

My husband, one of our sons, and I was about to have lunch when I had to leave the dining table to go to the kitchen, and as I was just a short distance off the right side of my husband I was alerted to look back at my husband, I did and saw that something was going wrong, then again I was informed in my spirit that he was going into a stroke and that I must hug him and pray for him, I did; and found myself rebuking the devil, and asking God to please touch him, and in seconds he was restored to his old self,

A few weeks later we went to Miami with one of our sons, his wife, daughter, and her niece, we left the hotel after breakfast to spend the day out doing whatsoever we choose, his wife and the two girls wanted to go to JC Penny so my son took them there, and parked until they were finish -my husband and I choose to remain with our son who quickly engaged himself on his phone -now and again adding a word to our conversation -suddenly my husband stopped taking part in the conversation which triggered my attention towards him who was once more being attacked by another stroke, I am fully unable to explain how I got him to the door on my-side, but I do know that it all happened quickly, and I found myself hugging him, rebuking the devil, and asking God to help him, and again in a short time the stroke spell was broken.

My husband and I have and will continue to give God thanks and praise God for always being faithful.

Experienced and written by: Corine V. Solomon

Manifestations of God for and through me -

"A Vivid Short Story"

In 1999 I started an oversea course of writing for short stories, radio, and television, from the NPIOA -I need to mention that back then I did not have any access to computer and I do not believe that back then anyone in the Western world had full access to online service -there by all correspondences were done Via airmail or fax.

As for the short story course I took only to obtain a Certificate just in case I ever needed it -as writing Stories, I do believe that I was given that as a gift, my first published book "Its Who." Was from 1986.

At this overseas school, my course teacher's name was Rose-Where. As the course neared its climax, one major requirement was to write what she called "a vivid short story." Unfortunately, by the time I received the assignment letter, I was dealing with a tough case of writer's block.

After rereading my teacher's request to write a vivid short story—and knowing I had limited time to complete and return it—I went alone into my garage, which is attached to my house. As it was already late, I turned on the light, sat at a sturdy white plastic table, and pleaded with God to help me, because I had no idea what to write.

After praying I humbled myself spirit, soul, and body in quiet worship before God in hopes that God would help me speedily, some time passed since I had prayed and I was planning to return to my bedroom for the night -I well recall that the spirit of doubt that God would answer my plea began to approach me -when a thought flooded my mind of a man who mistreated his wife and two children for years and by so doing had caused his wife to leave their home taking their children with her, after which; every sound he heard in his house, and even the voice of his next door neighbor's wife voice he heard as if it was the voice of his wife.

This ordeal went on for months until one day he suffered a heart attack. When he woke up in the hospital, his wife and two children were standing beside his bed. He begged them to forgive him and return home. His wife gently told him that while she could forgive him and would help in his recovery, she would not return to their home or to the marriage. I took notes concerning the thought of this story which was granted me and continued that late evening to convert that it into the short vivid story that my teacher had requested of me the first draft of 2.500 words was completing it in time to reach its destination on the appointed time, of which I gave God thanks for.

Approximately three to three and a half weeks later I received a personal letter from my course teacher asking me: how did I learn of his life that I was able to write it, and there in he abruptly informed me that he would no longer be my teacher, and also informed me that my course assignment would be turned over to a new teacher of which he stated her name, in a few short weeks the College sent me my certificate for short story Writing.

Experienced and written by: Corine V. Solomon

"After Nine Plus Years"

Mom told me that after my dad had made about three trips back to Grand Cayman from my birth country Guanaja of the Bay Islands of Spanish Honduras -he told her that he had met with some of his family in Grand Cayman, and some of them had advised him to return back home to Grand Cayman where he was born -in fact both of my Parent was born in Grand Cayman.

Anyway, my parents, two brothers, and I arrived on the island in July 1953—I believe it was a Wednesday. Though I was only six years old, I clearly remember the boat reaching the harbor very early, before sunrise. I woke up to the bustle of the adults and my mother getting us ready, giving us our cough medicine as we prepared to land. Being naturally curious, I scanned everything around me as soon as I reached the deck. I could probably speak for several minutes about all I remember seeing that day, but one moment especially stands out. As I was being led down the wooden ramp from the boat to the iron shore, I noticed a barefoot boy standing on the shore, fishing. My family and I were taken to a home in the Boswinbay area of West Bay, where an elderly man and his wife lived. We stayed there for about three months before Dad moved us to the Birch Tree Hill area, into a house where we lived until our own little home was built.

Like the majority of the homes back then; the kitchen was built at a fair distance from the main dwelling house, these kitchens were called cook-a-rum.

One day when mother were going to cook the family midday meal and dad and my two brothers were gone to work on the land where he was was planning to build our home mom told me to get my doll stuff together as I had to go out to the kitchen with her, reaching the kitchen I choose to set up my doll house under the white pine table that was next to the dresser where mother was working, playing the mom of my doll, I lay down with my doll to put her to sleep, and I guess you well know who first fell asleep -in that nap I had a dream -of which I learned years later that such is called dreaming, after all I was not quite seven years old.

In this dream I saw myself older like in my teens. I was-sitting on the floor in a cook-a-rum leaning against the east zink wall talking to my mom who was standing back on to me working at a dresser. I then saw a young man who I took to be older than me walk up to the door, leaned his upper right shoulder against the left side of the door frame, greeted my mom -who turned to her left and on seeing him she said: "Hi Tim! Its been a long time since we last met." sorry I do not have a seat here that I can offer you." then looking down at me he asked me if he could sit beside him, and after a look of approval from my mom he sat beside me and after some time he rested his head in my lap and I began to plat his hair that was resting a bit down his neck, then suddenly he got up and left the cook-a-rum, and suddenly I was deeply saddened by his leaving, and ran outside crying and searching for him.

I became full awake when mom caught a hold of me asking me why was I crying. "He left." I informed her. "Who left you?" She inquired, "the boy that came to the cook-a-rum and sat by me." "it was just a dream dear." mom said as she tried to explain to me exactly what a dream is.

Nine plus years latter that dream I had the day I fell asleep under the white pine table was all reenacted in our personal Cook-a-rum.

I learned later that Timothy -Tim for short had became a seaman from an early age and this day he had came to visit us on his return to Cayman, as he left that day I felt the sadness just like that I felt in my dream that I had under the white pine table - I then told my mom that he would be my husband, it was then that I fully shared with her all the information of the dream I had under the white pine table, but she did not accept that I was shewn that he would be my husband.

Tim and I was married on January 7, 1963.

Experienced and written by: Corine V. Solomon

"Needing Carpenter Help"

Having to shoulder the full responsibility of our renting business due to the attack on my husband's health. In 2022, I was in desperate need of a carpenter. I prayed and asked God for help while also continuing to search on my own. Though I often felt weary and my faith wavered at times, I held on, trusting that if it was God's will, He would send someone my way.

One evening, tired from a long week at our rented apartment, I got caught in the five o'clock bumper-to-bumper traffic. Because of the delay, I had to take a different route home. As I neared the junction to turn onto the main road, I noticed a man walking on the left side of the road, carrying something in his right hand. I didn't recognize the object at first, but just then, I heard that gentle voice, soft as a feather, say: "Ask him to work for you."

As traffic slowly moved forward, I rolled down my window and greeted him. I saw he was carrying a jigsaw box. "You're a carpenter?" I asked.

"Yes, madam, I am," he replied.

"Do you have a lot of work?"

"Not really, madam. I just finished a small job."

"Will you work for me?" I asked.

"I sure will madam."

I then gave him my phone number, and thank God I was once more blessed not only to get my work done, but again another reminder that I can trust God. Sometimes he may seem slow; but allow me to tell or remind you, dear sister, brother, family, or friend: He is always on time.

Experienced and written by: Corine V. Solomon

"Cayman Airways will Fly to Honduras."

As far as my memory recall, it was in 1987. My Parents and I was on our way back home to Grand Cayman on an aircraft of Honduras, a Lanhsa airline - reaching the airport in La Ceiba we learned that the flight to Cayman would be taking its route by first going to Belize.

The stay in Belize was very short, and we were once more on our way to Cayman -the flight had almost cleared from over the Island when the plain experienced a sudden shaking which last for what I think to be about fifteen seconds.

My mother and I sat together -I had the privilege of a window view, and my dad sat in the aisle seat next to mom.

The shaking of the plain brought a sudden fear over me, and I not wanting my mother to notice, I did my best to conceal it, and in doing so, I turned my head towards the window and engaged in a quick Prayer. Before I could reinstate myself, I heard a whisper deep in my soul which said: this will be the last flight of this plane to Cayman, and Cayman Airlines will fly to Honduras.

I did not at that time fully understand all the information that was shared with me then but what I did quickly understand was that the flight we were on would land safely.

It turned out that the aircraft never flew to Cayman again, and eventually, Cayman Airways began its route to Honduras. However, years before those flights began, I was once again in Honduras, having lunch with friends at a resort I recall being the Kimpton Grand. I overheard the owner speaking to one of the men in our group, saying how great it would be for his business if Cayman Airways started flying to Roatan.

At that moment, I remembered what had been shared with me on a flight back in 1987. So, I spoke up and told him, "Your wish will be granted—Cayman Airways will eventually fly to Roatan.

As the song I am now hearing says; "What a mighty God we serve." He has never made a mistake, and He never will Praise His Holy name!!!

Experience and written by: Corine V. Solomon

"A Message to two Brothers"

All of my family went home after Sunday school that day, but I stayed back for the midday service. While the service was going on, I suddenly heard a whisper, very close to my right ear: "Go and pray for Elsworth and Bobby."

I knew instantly it was Jesus speaking to me. Although I was an adult in age, I was still an adolescent in my spiritual journey and didn't yet fully understand the Trinity.

I began to struggle with how I saw myself spiritually. Questions filled my mind—why would Jesus choose me to do anything in His great Kingdom? Was it really Jesus speaking, or was it Satan trying to make me look foolish? If it was truly the Lord, why didn't He ask the ministers, Sunday school teachers, or the other helpers already involved in church work? If I was truly worthy, why had no one ever asked me to take part in the services before?

I always see myself as the least among the least of the least of God's Kingdom -many have told me that I degrade myself in so thinking, feeling, and speaking, but I ask: how can I feel any different? Will I ever feel any different? I do not for see it…

I am so glad that I have learned that when God calls anyone to duty -He equips them, and I am happy to also have learned that. He does not call the equipped, but again: He equips the called.

Before that midday service had come to a close -I was willing and fearless to go and Pray for the two brothers.

I went to the Church office and requested to be allowed to call my husband in doing so. I acquainted him that I was going to west bay, this I did without sharing with him the purpose of my trip, but informed him that I planned not to be there very long.

When I reached West Bay, I first went to Mr. Elsworth's home. His eldest daughter greeted me at the door, and when she learned, I had come to see her father, she led me to his room. I greeted him—he was bedridden from a stroke that had affected the entire right side of his body. She brought me a chair to sit beside his bed and seemed to intend to stay with us. After he shared the story of his illness, I told them that Jesus had asked me to come and pray for him. As soon as I said that, the young woman turned her left side toward me, and in that moment, I remembered the story where Jesus asked unbelievers to leave the room before He brought a young girl back to life.

I then asked the sick Brothers daughter if she believed that Jesus could heal her father, but without giving any reply, she walked slowly out of the bedroom.

On receiving approval for Prayer from Mr. Ellsworth -I held his left hand and said the words of Prayer that came to my mind, what all those exact words was, I do not recall, but I recalled closing by telling Jesus that all the honor and glory is His.

I then explained to the brother that the reason I was rushing was because I had to visit one more person—Bobby. I also mentioned that I had promised my husband I wouldn't be away from him and the children for too long.

Upon hearing the name "Bobby," he told me that Bobby was his youngest brother on their father's side. I was surprised to learn this, as in all the years I had lived in West Bay, I had never heard of any family connection between them.

Any way on reaching Bobby's parent home, where he resided with his widowed mother – I knocked on the front door, and as I waited for a reply, I began to feel an attack of what I would call sudden fear, but quickly I was assured that Jesus was with me, and I reinstated my mind on completing the job that Jesus had asked me to do, and just then his mother unlocked and opened the half screen door and invited me in.

As our greetings was over I asked her for Bobby informing her that I had come there specially to visit with him, she seemed to be a bit not too happy about I accomplishing that, and I know exactly why -as I had grew up with them being my neighbors, but it brings no glory to God for me to farther explain that, any way God saw to it that my mission be accomplished and in a short while Bobby had joined us around their dining table.

After chatting with him a little about the old days, I told him that Jesus had sent me to pray for him. I then extended my right hand to his mother and my left to him. Not long after I began to pray—and as I called on Jesus—I suddenly felt my left hand being crushed in his grip. A deep, hoarse voice came from him and said twice, "I am the only Lord—I am Lord Ababa."

In my spirit, I was crying out to Jesus for help. Slowly, I felt his grip begin to loosen. Then, as if he had just recognized me, he continued holding my hand—but gently this time. He looked across the table at me and said, "Hi Corine, I'm glad to see you. It's been a long time. Did you know I used to work for Cable and Wireless? Come, let me show you, my tools."

Not far from the table, on the opposite side of the room, he opened a small locker and pointed out his toolbox to me. I said to him, "You will work again, Bobby."

Seeing that his mother was walking behind us, I let them know that I had to leave and return to town.

Some months after that one day my mother told me after returning from her shopping in town: that she had met with Miss. Lilla Bobbys mother who shared with her my visit, and prayer for, and that the next morning before day

she heard him struggling, telling his father that he would. At breakfast, she noticed he had cut his nails and told her he was going to get his hair trimmed. At first, she thought he was only going out to collect the substance he had been hooked on for years.

But when he returned home, his hair was cut—and Bobby was back in his right mind.

As far as I know: he is up until this day still clean, and unbound from that which had him held captive.

A few weeks later my mother went to Merren store which at that time was located nearby where we lived, and on her return home she shared with me that she met Mr. Ellsworth within the store, and after commenting to him on how good he was keeping up in health. He then shared with her how he had been bedridden with a stroke, and then related to her the story of my visit to him three Weeks earlier and thanked God he was now well, and had regained his driver license.

I hope to one day learn that these two brothers along with me gave all the glory to God, and that they accepted, and served Him that they along with me may live in Eternity with Him.

Experienced and written by: Corine V. Solomon

"A message for a Sister"

One Sunday just like I did many a times over the pass Years -I quietly walked into the sanctuary as Prayer was being offered for the commencing of the midday worship, and as always if any way possible: I sat in the third row of benches on the left side of the middle aisle.

For some unknown reason to me at the time; my attention was drawn towards a sister that was sitting on the right hand side just about four or five benches from the front, on looking upon her my heart would be saddened after this occurred a few time in the said worship service I got concerned and pondered the reason in my heart – at some time that we rose to sing and my looking on her -I heard The Spirit speak to my spirit: "Tell her that her problem would soon be over."

Let me mention here: I knew very little of this sister, her first name -well, that which I heard the others call her, and the name of a brother of hers, also one day, someone pointed out her house in my presence.

I struggled a bit with sharing this message because of a personal issue—which isn't convenient to mention now—but eventually, I made up my mind and came up with a plan. I decided to go to the spot where I knew she would pass on her way to work at a shop in town. I followed through with the plan and met her there, greeting her with a "Good morning."

I called her by name and told her, "I have a message from God for you."

With a tone that sounded somewhat doubtful or even annoyed, she replied, "What's that now?"

I said, "He told me yesterday to tell you that your problem will soon be over."

Well -without revealing the other part of the story which I do not believe will bring any glory to God I will share what I know as the latter Part. In a few weeks after I had delivered the message to her: I heard that her husband -whom I later heard some long time afterwards use to be abusive to her -went on a boat and disappeared.

The repercussion of the message I delivered that Monday Morning brought me much mental harm, but thank God I have and am continuing to pray for all such like as is spoken of in Matthew 5:44.

Experienced and written by: Corine V. Solomon

"Even a Dress and a Pin."

Around the year 1997 or 1998 on a week day I was making ready to go to town to do some errands. on walking into my close closet to choose what dress I would wear my eyes quickly caught sight of my fairly new dress deciding that that would be the one I would wear, I began to remove the rack from the rod when I heard a gentle voice whisper in my soul "Don't wear that Dress." I ignored the voice thinking and saying to myself that it was only my mind I then proceeded to put on the dress and again I heard the voice. But proceeded to pull up the zipper which was in the back, and I having not as yet selected my shoes -I bent over to retrieve them from the rack below, and while bending over I felt the zipper slowly tear open.

Putting on my dress last and rechecking my hair have always been my pattern in dressing myself, it is no question to me on what would have happened to my dress in town.

The Zipper would have teared open and more than likely right where I would have been greatly embarrassed, Praise His Holy name for allowing me to waver from my pattern of dressing that day.

Yes -father cares about the smallest details in the life of His children.

Speaking on small details in the life of a Child of God: I also recall one Sunday not long ago as I made ready for worship service Putting on my Skirt and as I close the button in the band of my skirt and pulled up the seven inch zipper under it, I heard that gentle voice whisper "Put the pin in the band" and right there I understood that I was to support the button with the pin, and having over the years had become a bit more aware of His voice I reinforced the strength of the button with a safety pin, and as I went to sit on the bench inside the tabernacle the button burst in two leaving my skirt band supported only by the safety Pin.

I am so very thankful that we have such a wonderful Heavenly Father who cares about even the smallest detail in our lives, may we all always me keen to his voice, and always obey.

Experienced and written by: Corine v. Solomon

"Six Coconut Candies"

These were the years when I could not drive or did I have a car and there was no Bus service on the Island back then, so I, like so many others that had to do our errands on foot unless we were fortunate enough to own a bicycle.

For some reason that day it was paramount that I had to go to Town.

The family morning worship, my morning chores, and the preparation of the children's lunch were all done. I was fortunate to be able to leave the two eldest children in charge of the younger ones.

Before leaving, I firmly reminded them not to leave the house and assured them I wouldn't be long. As I pulled the front door closed behind me, I heard Timmy, my eldest son, turn the lock from the inside.

I was almost to the front gate of our yard when I heard these words whispered to me -more like right into my right ear than to my mind or soul: "Tell the children not to eat any food from anyone." Knowing through every fiber of my being that I had to turn back and tell my children, I did turn back and went inside, charging the Children as I was told.

On my return home, I found Timmy leaning with his back against the fridge door, when inquiring his reason for so doing he said: "Mom I do not believe that you had left long enough to reach the Gas Station when Miss. { I WILL NOT NAME THE WOMAN as she is yet alive and I will to win her to the Lord.} came to the back door and gave me these Coconut Candies, telling me that they were for us, so we must eat them." This he said, opening the fridge and removing a Paper Plate with Six Pink and White Coconut Candies, he added: "And the children wanted to eat them, so that is why I was standing against the Fridge door.

Without even commending him for his great guardianship, I took the candies from him and, along with the plate, threw them into the next-door neighbour's yard—intending only to feed them to her chickens.

Sometime after tossing the coconut candies, I heard someone say that the woman had claimed someone had poisoned her chickens. If it was the Coconut Candies that Poisoned her Chickens -God knows I did not mean to kill them, I only meant to feed them.

It is much more to this Testimony, but I feel it is not expedient and I do not see it bringing any glory to the name of God, but I will say: it is a dangerous thing for any companion to be unfaithful to their Marriage, as Satan's aim is to Steal, kill, and destroy.

Let me add with another effort to glorify God: my journey in this and many other ways has been -at times very rough, but I have been promised if I stay onboard – I will have a safe landed.

Written and experience by: Corine V. Solomon

"A Knock on my Room Door"

It was almost twelve a.m. one morning in 2016 when I retired for the night. I climbed quietly into bed, trying not to wake my husband. Lying beside him, I listened to the sound of his peaceful breathing. I must have drifted off not long after, because I hadn't yet heard myself begin to snore — something that often happened. Then, I was suddenly awakened by an unfamiliar knock on the bedroom door.

Upon hearing the unfamiliar knock on my room door, I was a bit alarmed but was quickly admonished not to speak or open the door, but I was quite aware that it was not just my husband and I in our bedroom. I kept still, and began to pray for how long I prayed I am not sure, but when I was awoken and learned that it was almost five AM.

I do not recall sharing this ordeal with my husband on that day, but I know I did so at some appointed day that Week in which the Unfamiliar knock returned before the day.

This time, I clearly heard the knock—and suddenly, I was drawn to look to my left. Standing in the corner near the foot of our bed was a woman I knew well. I don't recall making any effort not to speak, but I was so stunned by the sight of her that all I could do was stare. I looked at her for only a few seconds before she vanished from my view. I sat up on the edge of the bed, shaken, and that's when I saw it: from the very spot where the woman had stood, something began floating toward me through the air. It moved slowly—what looked like a dull, silvery block, about eighteen inches high. Its texture resembled that of cement. I could clearly see all four of its corners at once -one of which was pointed in my direction, I was then reminded to pray, despite all the thoughts that engulfed my mind: The only words that I could utter was "Help me Lord in Christ Jesus name."

I had only called for help two or three times when the block of what I later believed to be hot ice—began pressing its sharp edge against my upper body. It felt as though it was trying to force its way inside me. Strangely, I couldn't lift my hands to fight it off. Powerless, yet fully awake, I kept calling out to God for help, pleading in the name of Christ Jesus.

The battle grew heavier, and I longed for my husband to wake up and be with me. Desperate, I slightly turned my upper body and flung my right hand toward him, trying to rouse him. He stirred, but didn't sit up. Then, in an instant, I was thrown from the bed—landing in front of my ottoman, which sat near the bay window. As I hit the floor, my husband rushed to help me, but he could only manage to lift my head and shoulders.

I was then able to advise him to call the ambulance, which I did because of who I know he is. Therefore, I did not wish him to be alone with me -as I felt that this battle was not over, and knowing quite well that it was a spiritual attack and believing that more than likely it would retreat if I changed my environment, I was still crying out to God for help in only heavy groans- although I was not seeing anything just feeling the evil presencs.

Reaching the hospital, still in an midst of the battle, being only able to pray in my soul with only the heavy groans that could be heard.

Just a few minutes after being at the hospital, one of the Nurses attacked me, telling me that I must shut up as there were other Patients there beside me.

I wished that I had been able to explain to her that I was praying.

Experienced and written by: Corine V. Solomon

"Turn Left, Turn Your Head."

It was a Sunday morning in 1999, and my husband and I were up early, getting ready to head to Savannah to attend the 9:45 a.m. Sunday school class. I was the driver of my Grand Marquis for that morning.

"Put on your seat-belt, hon, as the life you save might be your own." This I reminded my husband just before I pulled onto the main road.

We had only driven for a very short distance when I felt like someone was sitting in the back seat of my car.

We had not quite fully crossed the south side of Hurleys supermarket when I felt the person in the back lean over to my right and whisper in my right ear, "Turn left, turn your head."

Obeyed the whisper, and just then—through the corner of my right eye—I saw a yellow car speeding toward me. There was no time to think, no time to speak. In the next instant, it crashed into the front right side of my car. From the assessments, it was determined that if I hadn't turned left, it would have been a full head-on collision. I know in my heart that it was God who had saved us from that. Later, I came to understand that this experience was allowed to happen for more than one reason—all of which brought glory to His name. I pray that it becomes a testimony not only for me, but also for the others who were involved.

Dear readers, I urge you—first of all, if you have not yet accepted Christ as your Lord, I encourage you to do so today. Secondly, trust Him in every aspect of your life. And remember: He honours His Word even above His name.

One of the greatest promises He has made to His children is this:

"I will never leave you nor forsake you."

Experienced and written by: Corine V. Solomon

"Results of the Faith of a Lad"

One night, after putting our children to bed, my husband and I sat in our family room cooling off and chatting before turning in for the night.

I was sitting beside the double window that looked out into our front yard, which received a little of the light from our family room and a bit from the nearby neighbor's house.

Off and on that night, my attention was drawn to someone moving about in the front yard. I pulled the curtains back a little more to get a better view of what was happening in the front yard. Not long after, I saw that it was one of the little boys from Jamaica who had recently come to visit. He was staying next door with his mother, who had moved in with her husband. The lad was walking slowly but restlessly up and down in the yard, my thoughts on his action began to bother me -so I decided to bring them to an end by first shearing with my husband what I was seeing, and that I was going to ask the child what were he looking for.

I opened the door and called the lad to come to me. As he reached me, I could see he was having trouble breathing. Still, I gently asked him why he had come over. Between short, struggling breaths, he told me that he had come to ask me to please ask Jesus to heal him from asthma. He added that my son Geoffrey had told him, "If you go and ask my mom to ask Jesus to heal you, He will. "Hearing this I felt so unworthy -I began to cry -My husband who was beside me at the time, said gently, "Corine, I'll get the oil for you. You anoint him and pray for him." Encouraged by his words, I pulled myself together and did just that. And praise God—that little lad received his healing from asthma instantly, just as Geoffrey had a few years earlier.

Oh! May we adults become as little children. Matthew 18 2 5.

Experienced and written by: Corine V. Solomon

"A word of Knowledge"

One morning during our family devotion, which I had just called to order, I must admit—I was planning to keep it as short as possible. The children were at risk of being late for school, and it also seemed like I would have to take them myself, as their father had hinted earlier that he might not have the time. While he was speaking to me, I had a very strong mind to tell him to check the bolts of the wheel of my car, I told him, but he did not.

Just after the opening prayer was over that morning, my husband announced to the children, giving his reason why he could not take them to school this morning, but that I would.

I then added: "I gladly will -but first, please do as I have asked you: check the bolts on my car wheels.

He then told our eldest son to check the bolts on the wheels. I wasn't pleased, as I didn't want him to miss the devotion, but I stayed quiet. Sitting beside the window, I caught sight of our son heading toward the car—just out of the corner of my right eye. When he reached the vehicle, he called out to his dad, asking which wheel to check. Since neither of us knew if it was a specific wheel, his father replied, "Check them all."

As I attempted to resume the devotion, I once again heard that quiet voice in my mind. Deep inside, I repeated the words I had first heard:

"The front left wheel."

Then I called out the window, "Check the front left wheel, son."

A short while after, our son interrupted the devotion by shouting,

"Mom! All the bolts on the front left wheel are completely loose!""Tighten them up, then check all the other wheels." His Dad added.

Once again, I give God thanks and Praise for his mercy.

Experience and written by: Corine V. Solomon

"A Pauper for a Night"

The experience I'm about to share took place during one of my trips back home to the Bay Islands, Honduras. As usual, before heading to the island, I landed in La Ceiba. On this particular trip, I decided to stay there for a few days with a woman friend and her sister. A cousin from the island had asked me to take one of her granddaughters to see a doctor, so I agreed to help.

The home where I would reside was for the sister of the friend I had traveled to Honduras with, so the evening we reached the house, I spoke to the owner of the house to conform approval for my stay, telling her the reason why I was staying over in La Ceiba for a few days.

She was overjoyed to have me stay and gladly she made me feel at home -showed me the room where I could sleep, which was the bedroom where her sister, my friend, used to stay whenever she was in La Ceiba. The room had two beds, and was quite nice and cozy.

The next mid-morning, my friend and I went to the airport and collected the granddaughter of my cousin, and we did all we needed to do to have a successful day.

That mid-evening, before my friend's sister left for her job, she asked my friend to take care of a few chores. One of them was folding the clothes from a few days' worth of washing, and the other was ironing some clothes that seemed to have been piling up for a few weeks. My friend told me that this was her sister's usual pattern—every time she knew they'd be spending time together, she would leave her with extra chores. Well, it was what it was. Anyway, I decided to pitch in and help. I started with the ironing while she cleaned the kitchen. Our plan was to tackle the mountain of clothes that needed folding and packing away. I remember hearing her call my friend upstairs to her room just before she left.

I knew not the contents of their conversation, which was very brief, but I well recall feeling troubled due to the call, and wondered if it was because I was in a new environment.

I kept my feelings to myself and thought about it off and on while ironing. I had started just a few minutes after her sister left for her 5 o'clock shift, and I finally put down the iron nearly three hours later. Just as I was about to place the last piece of clothing on the ironing board, my friend came over to me and, with a shy look, told me something that completely caught me off guard.

She said her sister had sent word that I—and the young family member who was with me—would have to leave in the morning because some of her own family members were coming in from Copan, and there wouldn't be enough space for all of us. That news hit me like the sudden death of someone near and dear to me.

I joined my young family member in bed not long before the young woman returned from work, which was after eleven O'clock.

My family member and I occupied the same bed, thank God she was sleeping peaceful, but that night my sleep was completely taking away from me, and my mind was completely captured with so many horrible thoughts -concerning the well fair of my young family member and I -I could even imagined seeing us being homeless, sleeping on the side walk without food, family or a friend reaching out to help us.

I struggled so hard to find a solution for the situation that we would be in the approaching day, according to the state of my mind, but there was no way out of this as I could not speak Spanish, which is what the majority of the people there speak.

I knew nothing more all night than that I was a Pauper.

Lying close beside one of the room's windows, I noticed the early morning light shining through the fairly thin curtains. That soft glare brought a sense of freedom to my burdened mind. In that moment, I remembered that I had money and also a credit card—I was more than capable of taking care of both myself and the young family member with me. God knows that I am unable to express in words the joy that flooded my mind that early morning, but I instantly fell asleep and was awoken when the family of the house was up making ready for their day.

After making ready, I called a Taxi to take my young family member and me to Hotel La Ceiba, where we aboard until we were ready to travel to Guanaja.

I pondered for quite some time of what had happen to my mind that night, and why, as this ordeal lasted for five and a half hours or more, and never one time did I remember to call on God for help, but why, as I prays about everything.

Praise His holy name! When my mind was freed from that dark dungeon that morning, I gave Him thanks and praise. I attempted to ask father what that experience was all about, but before I could complete my question, the answer flooded my mind: that I needed to know how it feels to be poor.

That experience has never left me. Since then, I've become even more compassionate than I always was, and I am now deeply aware of what it feels like to be a pauper. I thank God for this understanding, and I do all I can to help those who are less fortunate.

Experienced and written by: Corine V. Solomon

"Why and Who?"

My eighth birthday had just passed when, one day after lunch, my mom called me away from my play. She told me I needed to get ready to go to my sister's house to help her fill her water barrel. Mom handed me my paint can, which she had converted into a bucket, and sent me on my way to my sister's house, which was just beyond her brother-in-law's place.

My sister's big water barrel, which stood taller than I was, stood on an outside corner of her bedroom, which was the only room that was fairly complete within her unfinished house.

She had to cross the narrow path that lay between her house and the neighbor's where she had to fetch the water for house use, and bathing.

After many trips between the houses finally the barrel was filled, and the evening was well spent. It was far too dark for me to walk home even if I was allowed to -my sister having no one to take me home she told me that I would have to sleep over, that was all fine with me as I would get to spend some time with her little girl who was I guess was almost two years old, and her eldest half-brother on her father's side who was I guess about five Years old.

After our day was over, my sister placed her daughter and me on a floor bed at the top side of her bed, and her little stepson on a floor bed in the far south corner of her bedroom.

How long had we been asleep or what hour of the night it was I do not know, but the loud pounding on the room door that led from her bedroom to the outside awoke my sister, who must have been the one to unlock it.

Her husband entered in an unseemly manner but flopped into the chair on the right-hand side of the door in the room. I noticed that she was sitting on the side of their bed, and I knew she was praying. I must add, although I was just a young child, I could sense that she was graciously saved. At the time, I wouldn't have been able to explain how I knew this, but I could feel it deeply.

I clearly recall that it was then that I truly noticed how big her stomach had gotten, and I remembered hearing Mom say that she was going to have a baby. Suddenly, her husband reached into his shirt, pulled out a handgun, and pointed it at her, making threats. By the time the gun was aimed at her, I found myself standing between them, facing the gun. I remember speaking some words to him, though I don't recall what they were. What I do remember is that his head suddenly went limp, his chin resting on his chest, his right arm dropping to his side, and the gun falling to the floor. My sister quickly picked it up and walked toward the north corner, where clothes hung. I experienced the scene that took place between my sister and her husband, but I was sleeping on the floor bed with my little niece.

I don't have an explanation for why this all happened or who designed it, but I do know that God knows it took place, and it remains one of my childhood experiences.

Experienced and Written by: Corine V. Solomon

"Search for Casta"

Sometime in 1981, one of my male cousins and his wife, Casta whom my family and I had not met, came to Cayman.

Casta, who was from the settlement of Olanchito in Honduras, where the Majority of the people speak only Spanish, was not able to have a full conversation in fluent English, but her personality spoke for all she could not say; as it was as beautiful as she was.

I personally, over the next ten Years, became very acquainted with Casta and also her family, as she took me to Olanchito to meet them to share the story of all our active friendship would be quite lengthy, but is not convenient at this time.

Life became disrupted for both Casta and me, and we lost touch for a few years. In 1995, I took a trip back home to Honduras with the intention of finding Casta. I stayed at the home of a pastor in La Ceiba. After being there for a few days, I shared my plan with the pastor's wife, their eldest daughter, and a female cousin of the pastor. It was then that I made my plea for someone to accompany me to Olanchito. Both the pastor's daughter and cousin volunteered to join me on the four-hour journey. The next day, in early morning, the three of us boarded the first

Bus to Olanchito. On the bus, they both took turns asking me questions concerning my plan of finding Casta -the questions they asked were questions they should have asked before volunteering to go with me was which I thought.

All I could tell them was that I knew Casta and her family lived in Olanchito, and that God would help me find her. Their reactions to my only source of finding Casta weren't very encouraging. We continued on the journey, going through the familiar routine I had experienced years earlier. The only difference now was that the roads had been paved, which made the bus ride less dusty than it had been before. I kept my soul in prayer and humility before God for safety and success in finding Casta.

We had been out of La Ceiba for quite a few stops when a middle-aged woman got on the bus and headed in our direction in search of a seat. It was then that the Holy Spirit told me to ask her for directions to Casta Parent's home. due to I was not fluent in Spanish, I asked the woman accompanying me to ask that woman for the direction, but both of them reclined to aid me, I then reminded them that to speak the Spanish for me was the main reason I had paid their passage to come with me.

We continued our journey, and when we entered the bus terminal, I pleaded with them to ask the woman before she left the bus. Yet, they still ignored me. Once we had all disembarked, I pleaded again, but the pastor's cousin went to ask a taxi driver for directions instead. It turned out that the woman I had been hoping to speak to was aiming to take the very same taxi. At that moment, I decided that I would have to do my best to approach the woman myself, as I knew she was the one who could direct me to the family I was seeking. As I moved to speak to the woman, those accompanying me quickly stepped in, seemingly eager to fill in the missing pieces of the conversation. Once one of them managed to complete the question, the woman, with a joyful voice, exclaimed in Spanish: "Oh yes! Castita!" She then pointed in the direction of the home

I was searching for. I turned to my companions and confidently told them that she was indeed correct.

Was it that I fully understood what she had said, or was it that I recalled the whereabouts of the home? I am careful to say, but I know God knows; and also, that I knew that the Spirit had told me to ask that woman, and also that I found Casta's family that day.

On our way back to La Ceiba, the woman asked me how I knew that -that woman was the person to direct me. Well -that was another door opened once again for me to share the faithfulness of God, whom I have proven that were and still is faithful to His every Promise. I am truly grateful that God remains faithful, even in the smallest matters that pertain to the lives of His children.

Experienced and written by: Corine V. Solomon

"My Three Visitors"

On the North side of our new home stood a large, shady Poinciana tree, planted shortly after we moved in. Its long branches hung down like a waterfall, almost resting on the lawn beneath it. The thick clusters of leaves and light pink flowers, mingling with soft orange hues and dark burgundy buds, provided shade from the late afternoon sun and privacy from the nearby road.

One Sunday afternoon, I carried my lounge chair, Bible, notebook, and pen under the Poinciana tree with the intention of having a restful study session. After reading for a short time, I felt the need to relax instead. Turning onto my right side, I placed my books on the lawn beside the chair and lay still, listening to the occasional chatter of my family, the distant hum of traffic on the nearby road, the busy flights of airplanes overhead, and the birds in the tree, diligently going about their tasks. I tried to quiet the troubling memories and thoughts stemming from my troubled marriage. Gradually, I heard a nearby Russel as if someone had walked on dried leaves, and instantly, I was aware that I was not alone -by that time everything in my entire environment was as if asleep and I sensed that between the wall of my house and me was what I sensed to be three beings: one at the back my head, one like at my mid back, and another at my mid leg .I was not afraid but became highly Curious; and desirous to see those that I was feeling, but with all the strength and will I had I was unable to turn even my head, by this time my entire being was fully captivated by the profound peace, and quietness -which held me in its loving embrace for some time -how long did this wonder last-I am not aware.

I was gently brought out of this marvelous experience, as though I were a rosebud, captured in the delicate moment of its opening. Slowly, I began to hear the sounds of the world around me again. My three visitors, who had quietly arrived, left just as quietly, fading away in the same manner in which they had come. How much at this moment I desire, while sharing this with you -if I could even for a few seconds be captured in that world of peace and love.

Christ Jesus promises never to leave us our forsake us -I believe that He keeps all of His promises -although at time we go through dark tunnels of life -when we feel as if He have forsaken us, but such times are the works of the enemy of our soul.

Sister and brother, let us hold onto Jesus and trust His every Promise.

One may wonder or say that I was in a dream, under the Poinciana tree but God knows that I was as fully awake throughout all of that experience as I am now.

Experienced and written by: Corine Solomon

"Who, Lord?"

One early morning, after my children had left for school and my husband had gone to work, I found myself appointed to take action in a moment of reflection. This testimony comes from another act of God which took place quite a few years ago, but I am so glad that it does not matter how long the acts of God took place, the story of them will always seem to be new.

I was busy with my day duty when I was halted as I was told -I would say was: deep within my mind "Go and visit the hospital."

I tried to overlook the urge, as it was the first time I had ever encountered such a feeling. But no matter how much I tried; I couldn't shake the thought that I had to go to the hospital. But for what reason? Who was I meant to visit there? I pondered this all morning. After serving my husband his lunch, I decided to go. I made ready and drove to the old government hospital.

I went up to the double front door; paused and again wondered why I was there, I walked into the front corridor and again paused for a few seconds -this time right in front of the Nurses station, I was so glad that there were not any Nurses at the Station, because if there was and I had been asked who I came to visit -I could not have told them.

Realizing this, I looked down the corridor off to my right, and then to my left, not knowing which direction to go or who was I to visit so I asked: "Who Lord?" it was then that I knew that I was to go down the left side of the corridor.

I walked slowly, not ever pausing to peek into any of the rooms which were all on my right, truly hoping to learn who I was to visit, reaching the second or the third door right of the Nurses station I knew that it was in there was where I was to go.

As I entered the room, I greeted the woman lying in the bed, though I didn't recognize her at the time. She returned my greeting, calling me by name. That's when I admitted that I didn't recognize her. She then began recounting some past memories, reminding me of how my mother used to sew clothes for her. As she shared her story, my memory of her was fully restored. I then realized why I hadn't recognized her—back then, she was around 250 to 300 pounds, and now, in the hospital, I estimated her weight to be around 150 to 170 pounds. It was when I reached her bed that I was told in my spirit what to tell her, so I told her exactly what I was sent there to tell her, and that was that: "She must leave the hospital, go home and to drink tea made from Frankincense and Myrrh or she would die."

She then pulled back the sheet covering her body, revealing her left leg, which was severely swollen and purple. She explained that she and her sister lived together, and that morning, she had woken up feeling well. After getting ready to go to work, she stopped by the washbasin to brush her teeth. While standing there, her body suddenly gave way, and she collapsed to the floor. The doctor had since informed her that her leg was cancerous. She asked me if I would go and deliver the message to her sister, as it would be her responsibility to have the doctor discharge her. I was quite surprised when she revealed her sister's name to me, as for the many years that I was acquainted with her sister -who was one of the teachers at the private school where my children attended, I did not reveal to her, but told her that she would have to give me direction to their home which she did, and after the hospital visit was over, I went to the house and spoke to her sister after sharing the message. I was giving and had delivered to her sister in hospital, she too went on to share their suspicion of devilish work story with me.

I was given some advice for her, which I shared, reminding her that her sister was waiting for her to go to the hospital and have her discharged. Later, I learned that she never did go to discharge her sister from the hospital. Tragically, she passed away not long after. She too had neglected to do what she needed for herself, and her life was taken shortly after her sister's. Please note: I deliberately kept the names of these two sisters out of the Testimony, as there is still a family member of theirs alive, and I know not if revealing their names may cause an offence.

Experienced and written by: Corine V. Solomon

"A Three-in-one Blessing"

The familiar pains in my chest, jaw, and arm were back once more, and the doctors at the government hospital in Grand Cayman thought it best that I be checked by doctors at the Cedars of Lebanon Hospital in Miami. The Hospital provided a registered Nurse to accompany me and my daughter.

On the flight to Miami, we flew Cayman Airways -I chose to take the window seat, and my daughter sat next to me and the nurse next to her.

We had not very long taking our seats when the Spirit told me to bind an evil spirit that was on the Plain, I bowed my head and humbled my heart in quiet heart to heart Prayer to God, I then heard the Nurse inquire of me from my daughter who replied to her that I was praying, at the end of my prayer I whispered a binding command to the evil spirit in Christ Jesus name.

Our journey was just a few minutes underway when I needed to use the restroom. The nurse offered to accompany me, but I refused, assuring her that I wanted to go alone and that I would be okay. Reaching the rest room -I once again I offered a binding to command the evil spirit in Christ Jesus' name, this time I spoke a bit louder.

"Our flight thus far was wonderful, and when I looked out the window, I saw that the land was clearly in view. I knew that soon we would begin our descent. But in what felt like seconds, the plane suddenly rose and veered to the right. I would guess that we gained altitude again and moved about seven to eight miles away when the captain spoke, apologizing for the sudden maneuver. He explained that he had to take action because another plane was coming directly into our pathThe nurse somehow called my attention, and said: "Thank God somebody was praying." I replied: "Praise God He was listening."

I am persuaded that if God had not overruled -that evil spirit it would have distracted those Pilots and we would have been destroyed, allow me to once again give thanks and praise to God, and remind us: that He is The Almighty; and that He honors His word more than He does His all-powerful name.

"We reached the dwelling quarters on the hospital grounds where I would spend the night with my daughter and the nurse. As we entered the room, the nurse hurried toward the single bed, placed her luggage beside the head of it, and went to her knees in prayer. In her prayer, she first gave God thanks and praise for keeping us safe during the flight. I don't recall every word she said, but I truly believe she surrendered her soul to God that day They had me at the Hospital the next morning -by eight as requested.

I was taken to a cozy room with one door and one window, which was to the left of the bed with a chair beside it. A television was located at the foot of the bed, and on the right side stood a small wall table and a chair. After the hospital nurse finished settling me in, she informed us that the doctor would come shortly to speak with me and explain everything. She also assured us that no procedure would be done—if needed—until the next day After the Nurse left, my daughter asked me if I felt like I could do without her and the accompanying nurse for a while, as they wished to go to town for a few hours. I assured them that I would be just fine. On their way out, the nurse handed me the remote control for the Television and told me that I must relax and watch the Television of which she manually turned on -I thanked her and turned the Television off.

I instructed them to close the door; being aware that I was not alone, I engaged in heart-to-heart Prayer and once again recommitting my situation to Father.

I pulled my little Bible from under the Pillow from where I had placed it when entering the room, and decided to read while awaiting the arrival of the doctor.

As I held my bible in my hand before opening it, I felt a hand of fingers slowly rub my toes on my left foot, from the little one to my big toe.

I then opened my bible and it randomly it opened to Matthew 14: 27. While I was yet reading, the Doctor knocked on the door, and with my reply he walked in. He introduced himself and proceeded to inform me that my records from the hospital in Cayman show that I am having Angina, and he went on to explain what Angina is, and what the procedure would be to correct it. I then told him that I had been informed in Cayman that I needed a stress test, but the required machine was not available there. I added, 'God's will be done.' I don't recall his exact words, but I remember the arrogant way he responded to my mention of God's will. In that moment, every fiber of my being disapproved of him. He then handed me a clipboard with a form and a pen, informing me that I would have to sign it before the procedure could be done.

I then told him I was not signing it, he looked on me and left the room -not long after he left, another doctor entered and after introducing himself, sat in the chair that was off to my right. He went on repeating the same as the doctor before him, he went on to tell me that I needed the procedure done and that God would guide his hands, and I would be fine, when he finished, I asked him if he believed in God, and he replied: Yes - I do Mrs. Solomon without him I can't do anything.

I took the form from him and signed it.

The next day after the procedure was over the said Doctor told us that all test revealed that I had a blockage in some valve of my heart, but he did not understand what happened because when they finally checked everything, my heart was fine. Therefore, they didn't need to administer any treatment to it.

Brethren and friends, let us trust in the Lord, as He can do all things, praise His holy name!!!

Experienced and written by: Corine V. Solomon

"A Whisper in my Ear"

My husband and I left home early to be in time for the Sunday school class, as we had to travel all the way to Savannah, at that time, and our home is near Crew Road, which is just a short distance from the center of the Town.

I do not recall the month, but I'm definitely sure it was in the year 1999.

We were just a short distance from home, still on the private road leading to our house, when I noticed out of the corner of my right eye that my husband, who was in the front passenger seat, wasn't wearing his seat belt. "Timothy, it would be good if you put on your seat belt—the life you save may be your own," I said, with a bit of sternness. I had been reminding him for years to buckle up. At that moment, we were approaching the entrance to the main road. We drove in complete silence until we were almost past Hurley's supermarket when I suddenly felt a presence on the right side of my face. Then, I heard an urgent whisper in my ear that said, "Turn left, turn your head." I did as I was told, but I'm certain I had help in doing so. Through my right eye, I saw a yellow object heading toward us. That yellow object was a car, and we later learned that the driver had illegally overtaken the oncoming traffic. My car was crashed into on the right front in such a way that the Insurance said it would be written off.

My husband and I were taken to the Hospital, but Praise God we were saved from any serious injuries, and so was the driver of the other car.

But all that saw the crash well knew that if I had not turned to the left, it would have been a serious head-on collision.

Praise God He never leaves or forsakes us, and therefore He is a present help in time of need, yes, He gives His Angels charge over us, Amen.

Experienced and written by: Corine V. Solomon

"My Awesome Fall"

It was after Noon of December 19, 2022, as I was making my first trip to the bathroom since I went to bed some minutes after ten O'clock.

I got out of bed timely as always in an effort not to wake my husband, who I could hear was sleeping soundly.

I was feeling just fine and had finished using the toilet when I adjusted my pyjamas and took a step toward returning to bed. Suddenly, I felt as though I was being pushed all around the bathroom, which seemed much larger than it actually is. I was fully conscious, and I fought back hard against whatever was pushing me, trying to keep my balance. As I reached my dresser, which was to the left of the bathroom door, the right side of my face slammed against the wall above the table. In an effort to get away from the wall—or whatever force was trying to press my face into it—I straightened up a bit but suddenly collapsed to the floor, flat on my back, as if I were a wet blanket released from someone's grip. I recall knowing that my right arm was stretched completely above my head, with my hand resting against the doorway of my bedroom.

Then, I felt a hand placed between my lower back and the floor, turning me onto my right side. It was at that moment I realized that from my neck down, my body felt completely dead. I then heard a voice whisper in my left ear, saying, "Jesus, Jesus." I began repeating His name, though I'm not sure whether I was speaking aloud or just thinking it. I became acutely aware that I was not alone, and I longed for my husband to be with me. That desire was almost instantly fulfilled as he began calling me, trying to help me get up. When he had no success, he was soon joined by our live-in helper. I don't know whether he left me to go to her room to ask for her help or how exactly she knew we needed help, but I'm quite sure I never lost consciousness. I knew that he didn't leave me or call out for her, yet she soon came into our bedroom to assist us.

They tried to lift me but they were unable to. I heard them complaining that I was too heavy to lift. Then she took me by my arms and pulled me into the space between the foot of my bed and my bay window. She called for an ambulance, and went through all the procedures with the person on the other end of the line. Soon two male Paramedics were inside my room, but they too were unable to lift me I overheard them deciding to slide a flat sheet under me and roll me onto it. With this method, the four of them were finally able to lift me slightly off the floor and onto the stretcher, which was first lowered to its capacity. By then, I felt my body lighten up a great deal.

Reaching inside the ambulance, they found that my blood pressure, blood sugar level, were pleasing, but I think it was due to my blood Oxygen, skin color, and my body temperature that they proceeded to take me to the Hospital.

About a half hour after being in the Hospital, our helper who sat beside my bed, phone in hand turned to me and said: "Ma, you are begin to look better."

Just before the seven O'clock shift, I was discharged from Hospital.

Once again; I thank God for this another experience or lesson in the proof of His faithfulness, and the reminder of what He says in Isaiah 54: 17.

Experience and written by: Corine V. Solomon

"My Dads Departure Foretold"

My husband, three-year-old granddaughter Thresia, and I were doing a sleepover at the Marriott Hotel in Miami on our way back home to the Cayman Islands from our trip to Curacao, where I had been representing the poets of Cayman in 2000.

We reached the hotel around five O'clock, and being tired, we had supper in our room -as always on this trip, my husband and granddaughter watched TV, and I took advantage of the time to rest.

Thank God we had a good night's rest, but before day I awoke from a dream in which six numbers were involved, I quietly got up in an effort to get a pen or pencil to secure the memory of them.

My activity in the room woke my husband, who asked why I was up so early. I told him I had a dream, something that's always been very rare for me. He then asked about the numbers, and after I shared them with him, he said, 'They could be the winning numbers for the lottery. "Well

- if you wish to purchase them for lottery you are free to do so, But I will not." This I said because as a Christian I do not Gamble."

A while later that day, for some reason, the numbers from my dream came up in our conversation. It was then that I shared the dream with him, without revealing what I believed the meaning of the dream to be.THE DREAM: I was standing in front of a small house, with only one door which was open, on the left side of it was a large blackboard with a piece of white chalk and an eraser resting on the bottom of its wooden frame.

Just then, I saw a short woman walk through the door and stand beside me on my right. She was speaking to me, but I can't recall what she said. When I turned to look at her over my right shoulder, I saw a very large white bird, which I took to be an oversized dove, about the size of a white heron. It spoke to me, asking me to pass the chalk, which I did. The bird took it in its beak, went to the blackboard, and wrote the number two on the right side of a nine that had been on the board — something I hadn't seen before. "Write one more of them," the bird asked me; as it returned the chalk to me, I wrote another two, and instantly beside it appeared the number one. Five, and six, and there on the Black Board was: 922156.

After seeing the numbers I turned to my right, and noticed off in the distance a little white house and in its open door on the outside stood the big white Bird that was with me at the Black Board then instantly in its place stood a slim body man dressed with a white shirt and dark Trousers, I do not recall seeing if he were bare foot or not, but I clearly remember that he wore a heavy gray dress hat, he stood with his left foot up upon the door threshold -I noticed how erect he stood.

As I stood looking at the man, who felt familiar to me, a big lizard jumped onto my shoulder. In my effort to free myself from it, I fell onto my side and suddenly woke up from my dream about the big white dove. The meaning of that dream had already been revealed to me, but I lay still for a short while, pondering the meaning of the lizard. Filled with questions, I prayed and asked God to take care of it, as it had become quite a concern for me. Slowly and quietly, I got out of bed, trying not to disturb my husband. After all, it was around five in the morning, and I knew that when he traveled, he didn't sleep soundly, I walked towards the vanity in search of a Pen or Pencil of which I noticed was there along with a small writing Pad when we first entered the room. just then, my husband awoke and enquired. of me what was wrong "just looking for Paper and a Pen." I replied I had a dream and wish to write the numbers that was in it down on telling him; he inquired concerning the numbers, after sharing them with him he said; they may be the winning numbers for the Lottery.

Well -I will not be purchasing them.

The next day after we reached Cayman, I went to visit my parents and could not withhold sharing with my mother the numbers I had dreamt of, but was hesitant to share all of the dream with her. She, too, said that the numbers may probably be the winning numbers for the Lottery.

Well, if you want to buy a lottery ticket with it, it's up to you,' I replied. God knows I felt terribly guilty when I said that to her because, first, I knew she professed to be a Christian, and I am persuaded that children of God should not get involved in gambling. Second, I knew I had received the interpretation of the dream, but I was a bit afraid at the time to tell her that God was showing me the time of my dad's passing. Anyway - I returned the next day to my parent home Prime Merly to spend some time with my dad as he was partly bedridden, but before engaging in my visit with him, I called my mother aside and told her of the entire Dream that I had in the hotel in Miami and the meaning of the numbers. "Mom, Dad will go to the hospital on September 2, he will cross over when he is there on the third day, and his body will be put away on September 21."

With words I took as harsh, she replied to me, "Blessed Christ Corine -only God knows when anyone will die. "These words of hers pierced every part of my being, but I tried very hard to conceal my hurt and embarrassment.

"I know Mom, but God is my friend, and He has shared with me what will take place with Dad in the next three months."

It was the same day, while talking to my mother, that I learned my daughter Jacqueline had fallen out of a speeding jeep. Thank God she fell on her side. This happened that very morning, just before dawn, around the same time I had dreamed of a big lizard jumping onto my shoulder, causing me to fall on my side and wake up from the dream about the big white dove. I praised Him then for His care taking of my daughter, then and I praise Him now and will praise him forever.

God has never made a mistake and never will -therefore, things happened with Dad just as it was foretold.

I am so glad that, although Dad had a narrow chance, he accepted the shed redeeming Blood of Christ Jesus barely three months before he passed.

On that day, we took him to the hospital, and he was taken into the examination room. The doctor asked my mother, my sister Elma, and me to please wait in the waiting room. Once they finished checking on him, someone would call us. I sat between my mother and my sister in the waiting room, but after a few minutes I was stirred in my spirit to go check on my dad.

I excused myself and walked up the aisle that led to the half double doors, which opened to the examination room where Dad was. I entered and spoke to him, inquiring how his soul was with God. He slowly raised himself up on his right elbow, and as he began to speak, the doctor and two nurses entered the room. However, upon hearing Dad testifying, the doctor paused and stopped the nurses by extending his arms to both sides. I was so happy to hear my dad's first and last Testimony, which was: "I have asked Jesus to forgive me for all of my sins, and I believe that He have."

Amen and amen! Dad, the Word of God says, 'Let it be unto you according to your belief.'" I then recalled the big white dove from the dream, and my heart rejoiced then, as it still rejoices now, to know that my dad left this world justified in the eyes of God. Sometime after dad's funeral I was looking in on my collection of family pictures and, I came across an old black and white photo of dad. It was just as I saw the man who stood at the door of the little white house in the dream I had in Miami, and then realized that it was him standing at the door, and that is why I had the feeling that I was acquainted with him, I must share that when that photo was taken of dad, I was just a little Child.

I firmly believe that in heaven, everyone will be youthful.

Experienced and written by: Corine V. Solomon

"I Didn't Know"

If my memory serves me correctly, it was in the year 1985 that I opened a small clothing store in the last shop space on the far left end of A.L. Thompson Plaza in George Town. I named the business after myself—partly because the building owner's wife happened to share my name. On the left of my store better known as Corine's Corner, was a Toy store, the giving name of which I do not recall, but the storekeeper's name is one I believe I will always remember, as her name is Mary.

Every Evening at six O'clock, Mary and I closed the stores. sometimes we would sit outside and have a few minutes chat, sometimes before I would leave, Mary husband would drop in to collect her, as they had only one car.

"My memory does not grant me the exact month or day of the week when the incident I'm about to share occurred, but I clearly remember closing my store and seeing Mary seated outside, waiting for her husband. I recall telling her that I hoped he would arrive soon to pick her up. I hadn't been home for much more than half an hour and had just begun tending to my household duties when an unsettling thought crept into my mind:

that Mary's husband might not come to collect her, and that I ought to take her home myself. Knowing she lived all the way in the West End of the Island, I tried to dismiss what I called just a passing thought. But I wasn't doing a very good job of suppressing the feeling—perhaps because I've always been a people person. After wrestling with this feeling a few times, my mind suddenly shifted to a striking question: "Are you sure you locked your shop door?" I rehearsed the question a few times in my mind but concluded that maybe by stopping to speak to Mary I may not have turned the key. (God will never force any, but He can sure make us willing can He)

So then with this thought I acquainted my husband that I had to return to the store and asked him to feed the children and hold down the fourth till I returned.

Reaching near the store I saw Mary still sitting outside.

Upon entering the parking lot, I parked my car without turning off the engine and quickly hurried to check my shop door—it was safe and secure. Turning to her, I asked her what I realized later was an unnecessary question or statement: "Your husband has not come for you as yet." Come let me take you home, I said to her. She then reminded me that she lived in West Bay, but I assured her I would take her home.

As we made our way toward West Bay, she once again spoke about what might have caused her husband's delay in coming for her. Suddenly, a strong thought came to me, one I felt compelled to share with her—about how, as Christian women, we are called to live with faith and grace, even if our husbands are unfaithful, or even if they are taken from us by death.When reaching her mother's yard where she and her family lived, her three children were out in the front yard, and on seeing that their mother was in the car, they all ran out to meet her.

As they reached the car, her eldest child—her son, who was just about twelve years old—looked at her and quietly announced, "Mama, Daddy is dead. He drowned this evening."

Mary turned and looked at me for a few moments, her face clouded with a troubled expression. Oh my, I thought, does she believe I knew about her husband's death and chose not to tell her? She stepped out of the car without a word, and I, too, was struck speechless. Silently, she led the way into the house. I parked my car and went into the house in effort to try to comfort the family, but also to try to clear myself by letting her know that I did not know of her husband's death and in hope that she would believe that I was telling her the truth.

I spoke to her with a pleading tone, "I want you to know—I hadn't heard this news until just now." I repeated my words a few times, hoping she truly understood. Then, with a heavy heart, I took my leave before nightfall. I later realized how thoughtless I was of her responding to my plea, as I did not take her loss into as deep a consideration as I should have, of which I am greatly sorry.

I never recall that she ever replied to my plea of innocence of I knowing before we reached her mother's house -that her husband had died, and God knows that I didn't know.

Experienced and written by: Corine V. Solomon

"Another Attack from the Spirit of Hate"

In 1989, my husband and I went to Honduras for our medical check, having been acquainted with a Pastor and his family who had given us an open invitation to make their home our abode whenever visiting La Ceiba, we decided to accept the invitation.

Our medical appointments were scheduled for the second day after we arrived in La Ceiba. We attended them, and my husband was the first to receive his results. Since he had completed his part, he decided to return home and leave me behind to finish mine.

The evening before his departure, we were invited to join the Pastor on his front porch for a relaxed evening chat. During our conversation, I made an error—I shared a vision I had experienced in the tabernacle during the last meeting, which had taken place that Wednesday evening of the same week.

I have thought, was it a mistake or was it God appointed?

THE VISION:

"I saw the rostrum being shadowed with part darkness and part low light, and in the low light was a figure of a man fully dressed in black with a cloak and hood which concealed his face."

When I was finished sharing the vision with the Pastor and my husband, the Pastor asked me what I believed was the meaning of the vision.

I told him that I was careful to answer that matter, but God knows. I saw that his countenance was changed, and I thought it best to keep a low profile with him.

The conversation went on till almost twilight, as he and my husband chatted from one thing to the next.

My husband left to return to Cayman the next day, which was Friday.

Saturday was a fairly good day, and on Sunday I attended all of the Church services with the family.

Sunday night, after service, I sat at the dining table for the supper his wife had offered me, not long after I began to eat, the Pastor joined me at the Table to also have his supper.

Not long after we sat at the table, he asked me a question regarding one of the issues that had caused division in the church. Deep down, I sensed that he was trying to find out which side of the issue I stood on. As I had done when he asked about the vision, I gave him a careful, neutral reply.

He then instructed his wife to bring him his Bible. I could tell she was troubled—perhaps even upset—by his intention to challenge me. When he received the Bible, he opened it and began reading aloud, explaining passages as he went, clearly trying to show me the "truth" of the matter. I assured him that I was listening, but I chose to keep silent about my own point of view.

I greeted the family goodnight and turned in for the night.

Monday was the day I had to return to the doctor, and the pastor's wife accompanied me. On our way back home, she opened up her heart and unburdened her soul. She spoke of how, over the years, he had suppressed her—dismissing her every aspiration and belittling her desires. She even shared how he once told her she would never travel on one of the big airlines, something she had long dreamed of doing. This was as we walked home, and it was shared with me that that night, her husband had pressured her to tell him all that we had talked about, exactly how that issue was conducted, I don't know.

We all went to bed fairly late Monday night.

I clearly recall locking the bedroom door and windows, and after saying my prayer, I climbed into bed, lying on my stomach—the position in which I loved to sleep. I had only been resting for a short time when I felt something incredibly heavy press down on me, so heavy that I couldn't move. In that moment, I was reminded to call out to Christ Jesus for help. I did so, and within seconds, my body was freed.

But no sooner had I been released than I heard a sound coming from between the bed and the closet—like someone brushing their feet very hard across the floor. I resumed praying, and the room became quiet again.

Fear began to creep in, urging me to call for help from the family. But as soon as the thought crossed my mind, I was discouraged from doing so, so I continued praying for God's assistance. I tried to settle down again and turned onto my left side, but just as I was about to fall asleep, I heard the brushing sound once more at the foot of the bed. I immediately re-engaged in prayer, and once again, peace returned to the room.

Fully awake now, I felt an irresistible pull to open my eyes, and when I did, I looked toward the door. There, standing as if the door were open, was the silver skeleton of a man, one foot raised as if resting on something. I distinctly remembered locking the door and testing it. It struck me then that this too was the work of the enemy. In that moment, I realized my battle wasn't over. I was under another attack by a spirit of hate.

I continued praying, but my body, exhausted from the struggle, was in desperate need of rest. Realizing it must be well past one in the morning; I asked God for complete victory over this enemy and for the strength to fall asleep.

I saw that the tormentor in the door had gone, of course, the urge to call for help returned, I prayed on and knew not any more of the torments of the night till I was awoken with the high sunlight shining through the window curtains.

Thank God I was able to leave that home without revealing this ordeal to anyone, and this is the first time I have publicly shared it, and I praise His Holy name that no weapon formed against the child of God will prosper.

Experienced and written by: Corine V. Solomon

"Kidney Problem"

I was becoming so tired that I began leaning against the wall despite wishing for a seat as my back pain started acting up while I stood in line awaiting service from the Western Union clerk. I wondered why the other clerk wasn't on duty, which made me increasingly irritable. I even contemplated walking away, but knowing that the deadline to send the monthly donation money was approaching, I decided to stay in line despite the growing discomfort in my lower back. I quieted myself and called on God for help. All thanks and praise to Him for always being a present help in times of need. My endurance increased, and finally, it was my turn to be served.

I had just made my request of service to the young clerk when six words flooded my mind, and quickly I knew I was to speak them to the young clerk.

I turned fully to the round hole in the glass that separated the young woman and I, looking at her name tag, I call her attention and said to her: "You do not drink enough water." And looking up at me, she replied: "Yes, ma'am, I do not drink enough water." "But you should drink more water, dear, or you could get a bad kidney problem." She then shared with me that she had an attack from her kidneys a few years back. While she was talking, I was reminded that God loves her. I then told the young woman that God wished me to tell her that He loves her, looking up at me, I saw that her eyes were filled with tears, and I was made aware that the Holy Spirit was dealing with her.

After the transaction finished, as I walked away from the counter, I noticed that the pain and discomfort had left my body.

Praise His holy name! God never ceases to amaze me.

I loved Him Long before then, I love him now, and I desire to love Him forevermore.

Experienced and written by: Corine V. Solomon

"The Third or Seventh Heaven?"

It was a Sunday sometime in the 1970s at an all-day meeting in Savannah, where in the morning and evening service two of the elder Brothers did the Preaching, a brother from the North side of the Island Preached the mid-morning service, and the father of the present pastor preached the night service.

The brother who preached in the morning made a statement about God and the seventh heaven, while the brother who preached in the evening mentioned God and the third heaven. Though I can't recall their exact words, these contrasting statements about the heavens captured my mind with curiosity. I took this matter before God in prayer and fasting, seeking His guidance to reveal whether He resided in the seventh heaven or the third heaven. Back then I was not too much into the studying of the word -but more into the reading as I was a young mother trying to raise my children into the Nurture and admonition of the Lord, and not as yet having the zeal to be studious of the word, I prayed sincerely for months concerning this desired knowledge of where Gods abode is.

One morning, sometime before dawn, I had a dream that I am certain was given to me by God. In the dream, I found myself standing alone in an open field, fully aware of my surroundings, and gazing towards the East. Slowly, I became aware that I was no longer alone; someone had appeared, standing just behind my right shoulder. Before I could even turn to see who, it was, or if it was even possible to do so in a dream, I was told, "Lift your arms." Without needing any further explanation, I instinctively knew how to position my arms, as though this direction was being communicated to me without words, radiating from the presence beside me. I lifted my arms at a forty-five-degree angle, and to my amazement, I began to gently rise off the ground. I could still see the earth below me, and I was well aware that my guide was still at my side. After a while, as I floated peacefully in the air with my guide, I was told, "Look." I looked down, and to my astonishment, there was no trace of the earth beneath me. Instead, I was told, "This is the first heaven."

After some time, I was told again, "Look." This time, when I looked down, I saw the Earth, as if it were a globe. My guide then said, "This is the second heaven." Our journey continued, and gradually, my attention was drawn to what appeared to be a curtain of light grey, lined with dull silver. I couldn't see the beginning or end of this curtain in either direction. As we continued, I was slowly brought to a halt when my clasped fingers touched the curtain, and I watched as it began to open slowly, vertically. My guide then said, "Beyond this is the third heaven, where God's throne is."

Thank God, I later discovered that what I experienced in my dream aligns with what is supported by the infallible word of God—the Bible. I thank God for granting me the blessing to not only know that He is in the Third Heaven, but also giving me the blessing of a little peek of the heavens.

Allow me to here in slightly share a few words of my knowledge concerning the seventh heaven: Seven Heavens is a part of religious cosmology found in many major religions such as Islam and Hinduism, and in some minor religions, such as Hermeticism and Gnosticism, for a farther and quicker study on this search GOOGLE.

May we all be faithful in our Christian walk - so that we may one day live forever with God the Father, Christ Jesus, and the Holy Spirit in the third Heaven.

Experienced and written by: Corine V. Solomon

"How and Why?"

By the time I turned nine years old, one early morning, I was told to go to Miss Roseanna's yard and speak to the people about Jesus. However, I was instructed to first seek her permission. As I was receiving this guidance, I clearly saw in my mind the direction I was to face: my back was to be towards the southwest. I was also told to arrange chairs for the people to sit on, ensuring they were placed in a formation that covered the area in the East, West, North, and South. Additionally, I was instructed to select some hymns and Bible verses for the occasion. Back in those tender years I did not know about The Father, Son, Holy Spirit, or Angels. All I knew a little of was Christ Jesus, so to me, this voice was Jesus speaking to me.

The following day I got busy thinking about all I had to do to make ready to do what Jesus had told me to do.

I clearly recall thinking about getting a song book and Bible.

The next day, Mom sent me on an errand to purchase some item from Mr. Marvin's shop, which was very near our home. Just before reaching the shop door, I noticed one of Miss. Roseanna's granddaughter was walking fast, coming down the opposite side of the road. she then began to speak to me, saying: Corine, I will help you; I have already asked Grandmother if we can use the yard.

How does she know about what Jesus told me? I questioned. Because I did not tell it to anyone, but intended to ask her how she knew.

Standing there, I quickly realized that she wasn't heading to the shop after all—by then, she had nearly passed it. I knew too well that trying to call her back would be useless. Back in our childhood, when we were sent on errands, our parents would often say, "I'm going to spit on the floor, and you see that it doesn't dry before you return..." Those words stayed with us, a reminder of the urgency we were expected to carry in every task. I never did learn exactly all that the girl did to help me carry out what Jesus had told me to do. Back then, children rarely had the chance to gather freely. Most of our interactions happened during school breaks, in Sunday school, or if someone was fortunate enough to have a birthday party or be invited on a picnic. Opportunities to spend time together were few and far between, so whatever help she gave was quietly done, and I remain grateful, even if I never fully knew the extent of it.

Well -the time was near for me to go tell the people about Jesus, but a day or so before the appointed time, it began to rain and the rain lasted for three or four days, and as always, miss. Roseanna's front yard was knee high with water, which enabled us to get the job done.

I never was able to accomplish what Jesus had told me to do and for years I wondered why I was hindered but some years later after I learned of the Trinity. It was revealed to me that: It was not accomplished. I needed only to see that I was willing to do the work for Him and that the girl knew about what Jesus wanted me to do because she, too was spoken to by the Holy Spirit.

Some years later, after I had become an adult, I was having a conversation with a minister. During our talk, I was reminded of the calling I had received as a child, and I felt moved to share it with him. I told him about the experience, including the questions that had long stayed with me—how did that girl know what Jesus had told me to do, and why was I unable to complete the task?

However, I didn't tell him that I had already received the answers to those questions years earlier. When our conversation came to an end, he shared with me the very same answer I had been given before. As he spoke, I felt a deep sense of enlightenment—it was a reconfirmation, a gentle reminder from God that what I had heard back then was true.

Experienced and written by: Corine V. Solomon

"A Spirit of Hate"

I had met the eldest of my sisters-in-law, who lived off the Islands, only twice before a vacation my husband and I took to Tampa, where we were staying with our first daughter-in-law. I don't recall the exact year, but I clearly remember my husband turning to me one day and saying, "Let's take a bus to Orlando and go visit my sister for a few days. I told him that I was not interested in doing so, because his sister did not like me and God knows -for what. I did not know at that time, but he could feel free to go -I assured him that I would be safe, but he insisted that I come with him, assuring me that his sister did not dislike me.

Due to his deep desire for me to go with him, I agreed to join him in his visit .God knows it was just for the sake of peace. We left the next morning and reached Orlando just after Lunch and the day was spent at his sister's house in the fashion they choose to spend it. As for me I tried to keep in as cooperative spirit as I could, with hopes that she had changed her mind towards me since we had last met.

She graciously gave us her room for the night. I took the side of the bed nearest the door, while my husband lay on the side closest to the TV, which was usually her spot. I'm not sure exactly what time it was when I was awakened, but I saw a figure—some kind of being—standing where the door appeared to be open. Yet I knew the door was shut and secure.

This being seemed to be struggling to reach me, but something stood between us. There was a barrier—thick and flexible, like a kind of web—that prevented it from getting through. It pressed forward as if trying to get to me, but it could not. This continued until I called on the name of Jesus for help.The following day, I did not share the ordeal of my night with my husband because I believed that he would not believe me if I told him what it was.

In the early morning; he told me that we would spend one more night, and leave to return to Tampa the evening, it was then that I stood my ground and told him that I was leaving for Tampa -if he wished to stay, he could but I was not going to stay any longer where I am hated, and again he told me very strongly that his sister did not hate me.

As soon as everyone was up and about, he announced that we all would be going to a seafood restaurant for Lunch.

The four of us arrived at the most popular seafood restaurant just in time to catch lunch in its first bloom—when the dishes were freshest, the atmosphere lively, and the service at its finest.

My husband, his sister, her youngest daughter, and I sat at the first table on the right-hand side of the large dining room. As we waited for the menus, the three of them began chatting casually. Then, without warning, his sister suddenly looked across the table toward me and, in what could only be described as a gross, hoarse voice, said, "I HATE HER."

Startled, her daughter immediately asked, "Mama, who are you talking about?"

She pointed directly at me and repeated, "HER."

I turned to look at her daughter, then at my husband, who appeared to be in speechless shock, unable to process what had just happened.

The lunch was eaten in almost complete silence after which she and her daughter left for the rest room, I then asked my husband to wait inside for me till I was out of the rest room which I had planned to use when they were out He did and I heard her daughter inform him that they would wait in the car.

As I exited the restroom, I gently pulled my husband aside and told him that I had already packed our bag before we left his sister's house. I reminded him that I intended to return to Tampa as soon as we could retrieve it. He quietly agreed, and we made our way back.

During our journey, he admitted that he never believed his sister hated me—until he heard those very words come from her own mouth. It was then that I felt it was time to share the full story with him: the truth about the hateful spirit that had taken hold of her, rooted in her deep-seated colour prejudice.

Thank God, I never hated her, but I do hate evil spirits of any level, and if there is any way that I can avoid them, I have and will.

Let me add this from my heart: if you are a true child of God and you trust Him, there is no evil from which He cannot protect you. There is no good thing that you truly need that He will withhold from you. And whatever you need to know—if it is His will for you to know it—He will surely teach you.

Please, always remember: He is the Almighty, and He is the Father of all the righteous. Trust in Him, for His love never fails.

Experienced and written by: Corine V. Solomon

"A Miracle for a Sinner"

Was it a direct call from God, or did God just permit my desire? You are free to make your assumption.

Visiting the area of Watler's Road in George Town, in the Cayman Islands, where we had raised our children, and learning that the young children there were growing up without learning about God, I opened a Sunday School in the front yard under a tent constructed from lumber and a large blue canopy.

The little work had not long started when the majority of the children of that area were attending, and sometimes some of my Tenants, a few nearby neighbors, and a male and female Police Officers joined us in worship.

Among the group that attended was a young woman who had been faithfully present for a while, but her attendance was short-lived. Naturally, I became concerned about the reason. In finding out more, I learned that she was in a relationship with a young man who lived nearby and had become pregnant. After that, we only met occasionally when she came by to pay her rent. The end of the three Years that I labored there was almost to the end.

The children in Sunday School classes and Friday Night Bible classes, and the five adults that was attending had desired that I have Bible study for them, which took place on Tuesday Nights. Thank God my mom was among the Adults Bible Study. One of the adults who attended accepted Christ as her Savior, and mom accepted that it is only the Doctrine of Christ Jesus that we must live by to please Him.

"A few days after the 2005 hurricane, I returned to check on the condition of the hall that my husband had built for me to carry out the Lord's work. As I was leaving the yard, I ran into the young man who was in a relationship with the young woman — my tenant — who had once faithfully attended Sunday school. I asked him about her, and he told me that she was in the hospital, where she had just given birth to their daughter. I then asked him to pass on my well wishes to her. The very next day, unexpectedly, I had to attend the outpatient area of the hospital. And were sent to the X-ray department, in the passage way I saw the young lady laying on a bed awaiting her turn to enter the X-ray room, and in chatting with her I learned that the normal reaction of child birth had not taking place with her, but had traveled to her Stomach, and that was the reason for her approaching X-ray.

The next morning, I felt a strong prompting in my spirit to go to the hospital to visit and pray for the young woman. I arrived at the hospital by eleven o'clock, which was the first visiting hour of the day. After a bit of difficulty finding her, I finally located the young woman's room. When I entered, the young man — the father of her daughter — was sitting and chatting with her. I took the spare chair to the left of the door. As soon as I sat down, she exclaimed, 'I've been asking God to send me a Bible.' I pointed to the night table beside her bed and told her there was a Gideon

Bible there. But she quickly clarified, saying she meant someone who knew the Bible. Then she added, 'Thank God for answering my prayer and sending you.' Her words made me feel a bit embarrassed, as I felt unworthy of such an honor. But in no way a shame of the word of God.

She then informed me that the doctor had planned to perform surgery the following day. I then informed her of my reason for visiting her -she was willing and seemly eager for me to pray for her, I turned to the young man and inquired of him if he believed that God can heal. He politely assured me that he did, just then nature made a call on me, turning to the young woman, I asked her if I could use the restroom.

"While I was in the restroom, I quietly turned to God, asking for His blessing on the prayer I was about to offer. As I continued to pray, a sudden thought struck me—I had forgotten to bring my anointing oil. I felt a bit unsettled, but as I looked around, I noticed a small Dixie cup beside the basin. Then I heard a still, gentle whisper say, 'Put some water in it and dedicate it to God.' I did just that. When I returned to her bedside, I explained why I was using water instead of oil. Then, in faith, I anointed her in the name of the Father, the Son, and the Holy Spirit. My visit was over, and I left for home. On my way nearing the first traffic light, I had a flash vision of the young woman in the restroom and her body released what was due to happen after childbirth.

The next day I recalled that I had to check on her, but decided to wait until later that she would have been returned from the operating Theater.

I stepped out onto my back porch to cool off after the morning chores, with my portable phone in hand. It was around ten-thirty, or maybe even eleven o'clock, when I decided to call the hospital to check on the young woman. The nurse who answered assured me that she was in her room and then transferred my call to her. On hearing my voice, she south of screamed out calling my name, and she went on to inform me of what took place just after I left the hospital and added that the doctor had discharged her.

I praised the Lord for his healing touch on her body and admonished her to accept Christ as her Savior.

From the moment of visiting her in the hospital, I have never seen or heard from her.

Experienced and written by: Corine V. Solomon

"A Brush with Death"

"Our youngest son, Loxley, joined the Cayman Islands Police Force at a young age — a decision that neither his father nor I was entirely pleased with. However, we chose to honor his choice of career. Once again, we prayed for his safety and rededicated him to the Lord. Not that we had ever taken back our first dedication, but this act was our way of reinforcing our desire for God's protection over his life. He was only seventeen years old when he made this move in 1993 and was accepted as a Cadet due to his age, he was given his regulation number at age eighteen.

He served in that rank until 2006, then in 2017 he was promoted to Sergeant, while in this rank, one early morning, while still at home, he was called out for duty on the task of locating and capturing a Prisoner that had escaped the prison.

"As he was getting ready to leave for duty and face the task ahead, he told me he heard a deep inner voice whisper, 'Put on your bulletproof vest.' he said At first, he ignored it, thinking it was just his imagination. But as he was about to walk out the door, he heard the voice again—this time, it was louder and more firm: 'Put on your bulletproof vest.' So, he returned to his bedroom and put it on, though somewhat reluctantly. The prisoner was soon apprehended, and the chase was on which led to unfamiliar paths to Loxley, therefore he fell over a foundation which had been engulfed by weeds, and thereby he fell on one of the steel rods that were protruding from one of the blocks in the foundation which in his fall was directed right to his mid chest but was brought to a halt by his bullet proof west.

Now that was a Brush with death, wasn't it.

Must we question what would have happened if he had not put on his bullet proof vest?

Praise God for His watchful eye over him, and for aiding him to obey His voice!!!

Parent God has loaned our offspring to us -I admonish us all to give them to Him to lead, guide, direct, protect, and save -as He is fully able to do all this along with all they can ask or think.

I have fully dedicated or given all my offspring to Him, if you have not already done so – I admonish you to do so today.

I heard this true story directly from our son himself. He was later promoted to Acting Inspector in 2017 and eventually retired from the force in 2019."

Experienced by: Loxley Solomon. Written by: Corine V. Solomon

"Angels on Amtrak"

A PEEK IN ON OUR TRAVEL:

I deeply regret giving up keeping a diary or journal for many years. However, if my memory serves me correctly, it was in 2002 when my husband and I attended a camp meeting in Virginia. Afterward, we decided to journey back home via Miami. Since we had never taken a train ride before, we chose to travel by Amtrak and then take a flight back home to the Cayman Islands.

We were on time to catch the first train out that morning. We purchased First Class tickets, which would provide us with a cabin, as we had to travel through the night. This we learned at the ticket counter, where we were also informed that the journey to Miami would take until four the following evening. A couple from Tampa, with whom we became acquainted at the Campgrounds, were also taking the train back home, but they decided to take the coach, as their journey was much shorter.

We were escorted by one of the train attendants to the neat, cozy little cabin where we would spend the night. We placed our two pieces of hand luggage beside one of the broad, sofa-like chairs. Our escort closed the twenty-inch sliding pocket door and then gave us a brief tour of the small cabin. Afterward, we spent a few minutes getting more acquainted with our little space. On the right corner of the door were a communication gadget which consisted of a Phone, intercom, and a Radio, on the wall -beneath it was a small corner like Table with a little seat attached to it, and in the left corner of the door were a neat varnished wooden box with a lid, lifting the lid revealed that it was also the toilet, which also served as a step up for the upper bunk.

On the main wall were the two sofa chairs where our hand luggage was leaning against -they folded into a bunk bed, and alongside each of the chairs was a little Window about eighteen inches high with neat little curtains that could be pulled to each side, between these windows were a horizontal slot in the wall about twelve to fourteen inches long, from which a small Checkered game Table nestled and could be pulled out.

I then reminded Timothy that it was high time to engage in prayer, which we did with our cabin door open. A short while after, we heard some noise in the passageway that separated the cabins. I was sitting at an angle that gave me a better view of the passageway from where the noise was coming. Timothy, curious, inquired about what could be causing the noise. I informed him that it was an atheist male who had dragged a suitcase into the cabin on the other side of the passageway.

An Atheist, Timothy repeated, I then thought for a while on what would cause me to say that. "Yes, hon; an Atheist a person who does not believe that God is God."

Timothy pulled out the game table and set up the game without saying anything more about our next-door neighbor, which I was glad about. He then announced that we would play the game while waiting for our call to lunch. Of course, I tried to get out of it, since I'm not a game person, something he was well aware of. But after he pleaded with me to try it—telling me he would teach me and assuring me that once I learned, I'd love the game—God knows I knew I wouldn't, but despite that, I granted his wish, as there were no other options anyway. He taught me the game, and to my surprise I learned it quick, but to get the interest in playing it -of course was a remaining struggle, but despite that -we engaged in playing the game -well as expected he won three rounds straight, and I refused to play anymore.

Lunch was over, and we were well on our way to Miami. we soon gave up on our efforts of trying to catch a pleasant view of the scenery as they all were, of course, passing by too quickly. I then regretted that we had not travelled on Greyhound instead.

We made the best of the balance of the day praying, reading, and chatting about the past and making plans for the rest of our stay and travel back home.

The call for Supper came in around six thirty or so, and on our return to our cabin we resumed our entertainment of the evening until Timothy became sleepy -as he is usually the first of us to get that call, so taking the overhead bunk, he was soon asleep, and I could hear him puffing in sleep -thank God on like me he rarely snores.

ENCOUNTER WITH ANGELS:

Finally, I made my way to bed. How long I was asleep, I know not. I was awoken—at least, that's what I thought—by what seemed to be the train running over large objects, causing a very rough ride, as though the train might lose its balance. That ordeal was soon over, but then a smell, which seemed like burning rubber, filled the cabin. 'I'll use the intercom and call for help,' I thought. But before I could turn to my left side toward where the system was, I saw a gigantic, beautiful angel standing outside on the south side of the train.

He hung his head over the north side, with outstretched wings that covered both the front and back ends of the train. I then thought, 'Lord, only one angel?' Instantly, I was convicted of that thought and quickly repented, asking God to forgive me. With a contrite heart, I added, 'O Lord, if they are this size, I only need one.' I cried this out loudly in my mind, and as I repented of what I called an unthankful thought, I was fully aware that God heard me, accepted my cry of repentance, and granted me forgiveness. I was called by a man standing in our cabin door, although knowing that Timothy had closed the door, and placed the safe on -I arose from my Bunk and saw standing in the open doorway a handsome man with his arms slightly risen but fully outstretched with the palms of his hands resting flat against the door frame. I would chance to say his stature was approximately three to five inches taller than I am.

In the early stages of this experience, it was impossible for me to describe his features or even his hairstyle. It wasn't until a few years later that I was able to do so. One day, while browsing YouTube in search of sermons, I came across some messages and pictures of Brother Charles Spurgeon. One of those images immediately caught my attention—I knew without a doubt that this was the man who had stood in the doorway of our cabin on the train. In that image, he appeared to be in his early thirties. As for the color of his apparel, I find it difficult to describe accurately. In all my seventy-seven years, I have never seen a color quite like it. I'll try my best: the design of his clothing resembled a full, roomy yet perfectly fitting jacket suit. The color was something like a brilliant yellow mixed with freshly polished gold, as though there was a soft light beneath it that hadn't fully shone through.

This man talked to me; for some time but from all of which he told me -I am only able to share what he told me concerning the approaching accident that the Train would encounter, and assured me that there would not be any hurt to any one, by this time I would say: I was fully calm, and engaged to being myself, so I inquired of him if the Train would derail, and he replied: "No the Train will not derail", I was at that time deeply stirred to look over his shoulders -so I tiptoed to take a peek although not being able to use the full capacity of my eyes due to his height. I saw a quire of people sitting in the back of him, in reality where they were sitting were all cabins -anyway I noticed that they were all dressed in the said color garments as he was, in the many things thing I have recalled concerning this ordeal is me taking that peek over the man Shoulder -I realized sometime after this experience, that he stood allowing me to do so -as my chin to rest on his lower right shoulder while taking the Peek, and another thing: -since the fall I had on a Republic Airline Staircase in 1986 -at what time I damaged my Spine -I was from then and still is unable to tiptoe.

"Anyway, the visitor who stood in the doorway of our cabin on the train gently informed me that he had to leave. I turned around—and to my surprise, I realized I was still in bed, lying on my right side just as I had been when I first went to sleep. I reached up to the little window in front of me and pulled the curtain slightly open, only to be greeted by darkness, occasionally interrupted by fleeting lights from passing buildings and other structures. I then grew curious about the time and checked my watch—it was a few minutes past three in the morning, though I can't recall the exact time. Sadly, I don't have a diary or journal to turn to for confirmation, and I deeply regret not having kept one for so many years. I lay still for a while listening to Timothy puffing as he slept soundly, as if keeping rhythm with the sound of the Train.

Thank God I awoke again at day-break, and quickly recalled the ordeal that had taking place earlier before day, after breakfast we had morning devotion with the cabin door fully open, aiming not to become bored, I decided to share my experience with Timothy, but just a bit after I reached the part where the man told me that no one will be hurt Timothy began to cry, "Remember hon -the man said no one would be hurt…I made an effort to try to comfort him when I was halted in my spirit to say no more, I kept quiet; and then I heard: "I washed his eyes with tears." Sometime later, I inquired from Timothy why he cried on the train -he told me that he experienced a profound Peace, and he assured me that this was the only way he could explain his experience.

We resumed our morning entertainment and were fully engaged in it -as far as I recall, he was engaged in his seek-a-word book, and I was reading when suddenly the train began to experience the said thing as I had experienced before day – "This is what I felt hon." I said, then suddenly mingled with what the train was going through came that smell of burning Rubber. "This is what I smelt, hon." By this time, the train had stopped, and the Train crew were running from cabin to cabin inquiring of the passengers, all around the Train were Police Cars, ambulances, and news investigators. we heard a helicopter over-head.

We soon learned that our train was on the main Railroad track, and that the front engine of the Train was damaged.

After viewing the outside commotion, we went back to our cabin.

We were sitting and chatting, making plans and adjusting for our journey back home—just in case we experienced any delays. That's when the man I had seen earlier—the same one who had noisily entered his cabin before we left the train station in Virginia—came to our cabin door. Without hesitation, he began speaking, telling us that he was a chartered accountant. He explained how he had recently met a very wealthy man who offered him a job with a tight deadline. If he could get to Miami and complete this important task in time—though I can't recall the exact details—the man had promised to pay him ten thousand dollars and take him on vacation to an island in the West Indies called Grand Cayman.

Then, turning to me, he said, "Please madam, would you pray that I get to Miami on time? I must be there by four o'clock to get that job done."

My dear readers and listeners, while this man was speaking—praise God!—I was given the words to say. When he finished, I gently told him, "Sir, as for praying for you—I am already a step ahead of you. I began praying for you from the moment you entered your cabin. And yes, we will reach Miami at the appointed time."

I do not know what happened in that man's life after that. I never saw him again, except for one last glimpse when we arrived in Miami at exactly four o'clock that evening. I saw him running out of the train station toward a taxi. My belief is that through this experience, God did something meaningful in that man's life.

It was at the Miami train station that I also learned the train had been pulling ninety-five coaches.

I said then and I say now, and by His grace I will say for all eternity: "What a mighty God we serve."

Someone asked me concerning this experience: "Do you believe that you were in the flesh or the spirit when you had this experience?"

To be thoughtful towards you my readers or and listeners: I have to say: we all are our free agents granted by God Himself -so your belief be unto you, and for me I just thank and Praise God for being my ALL and ALL to me, and there in never leaving or forsaking me.

Be I in the flesh or in the spirit, I wish to always be His.

Experienced and written by: Corine V. Solomon

"Born for a Great Purpose"

In the year 1999, in the Month of December, I had a dream one Morning before day. Now dreaming is what I would call rear in my life, but I thank God when they do occur, the majority is given for a purpose.

Returning to the dream I had in December 1999—our second son, Ellio, who at the time was the father of two young daughters, came by our home one evening for a visit. As usual, he and his dad quickly became absorbed in conversation, as they often did. So, I gently interrupted and said, "Bo, before you leave, I would like to tell you something very important. After the dad and son time was over, he and I met at the dining table and were quickly joined by my husband. "Well, Mom -I'm here at your disposal, waiting to hear your important statement." "Well, Bo, I had a Dream I need you to hear." "Oh, it is one of those again." He said kind of reluctantly; then looked across at his dad, who was samed to be all ears -he then gave me undivided attention. "The dream Mom, I am listening." He said, tapping his fingers lightly on the Table.

"Well," I began, "I had a dream just a few mornings ago. I dreamt that I was standing in the living room of your home, and in front of me was a long wooden platform. On it—off to my left—stood Samantha, and to my right was Sydney. I quickly noticed two things: first, they looked much older than they are, and second, there was a large empty space between them.

Then, all of a sudden, that space was filled. Lying there between Samantha and Sydney was a younger girl, stretched out on her right side, with her right hand tucked under her head, supported by her elbow resting on the platform."

As I finished, a quietness began to settle around the table.

"Was that all to the dream Mom?"

"The dream; yes, that was all the dream."

"So do you have any Idea what it was all about, I mean: what you think is the meaning, Mom?"

"Well -Beth will have another girl child, and…"O no she won't" he interrupted. "at least not if I am going to be the father."

"Slow down Bo; slow down and listen to me, if this is of God, we cannot change it, if not, it will not come to pass."

"But as I was saying: the child that Beth will have will be a girl and…."So what you are saying is that you truly believe that the dream was: God sent?" he once more interrupted.

"Please hear me out." I pleaded. As I tried once more to bring my speech to a climax.

"Please just as the child Navel string have dropped: secure it in something safe that dogs or cats will not be able to smell, berry it deep between the roots of a growing tree -One that you will never ever cut down, and then take her to the beach and bath her in the salt water."

He then began to question: "What would all that you said have to do with the child?" and he went on a bit more with words I do not recall, but all was of a sort of grave spirit.

In the late part of March 2000, on one of his Visits, he announced to his father and me that he wished to meet with us for a bit. We gathered around the dining Table to listen to what he wished to say.

"I wish to let you all know that I have decided to marry Betsy as she is Pregnant with our third child."

"Well, I think that is good, son; as you all have been together long enough to know each other." His father replied.

"At least you all will be out of the sin of fornication," I added with congratulations, and inquiry of the set time and where the ceremony would take place.

He assured us that as soon as all was organized, he would give us ample notice that we could be there.

"Bo -do you remember what I told you about this child three Months ago -in December of last Year, to be exact?"

He was puzzled for a while, then replied: "What you told me about this child? No Ma -I do not recall you telling me anything about this child."

At his reply, I do not recall if my state of mind was doubtful, shocked, madden, saddened, or what, but anyway I repeated exactly what I had told him right at the said table in December of 1999 concerning the child.

Their Wedding was small, but all went orderly, all thanks to God.

Beth came by our house eight months later, and during our conversation, she told me that the baby was due the following month—November 2000. I then asked her if Ellio had told her what I had shared with him about the baby. She assured me that he had never mentioned anything I had said. So, I went on to tell her the entire story myself and pleaded with her to follow what I had advised—because by then, it was clear to both of them that it was truly God-inspired.

The baby arrived on November 1, 2000, a beautiful, buncing baby girl, and she was named Shawn =I call her Shonie.

I was told by the maid of their home, who had heard the story concerning Shawn, who was then eight months old, that her navel string was still knocking around her parents' Bedroom.

It was that said day that I learned that she was not striving as she should, as she did not even have active motor skills.

Horror began in my son's home when Shawn began having seizures at a very early age, of which I think was as early as when she was fourteen Months old.

A short time after she began experiencing seizures, her parents were financially able to take her to a doctor in the United States. After conducting many costly tests, the doctor told them that he couldn't find anything medically wrong. He said he couldn't pinpoint what might be causing the seizures in the child, but advised them to bring her back when she was six months older.

Not finding anything wrong with the child, but to take her back in six months, that statement bothered me for some time, but after realizing that maybe the doctor was in hopes that whatever was causing the seizures may surface as she grew older -that settled the bother in my mind concerning that.

One day I went to Ellio's home and admonished his wife and him to add Sprat Tea into Shawn's daily diet.

"You get the Sprats' son; and I will teach Beth how to make the tea." This Sprat tea recipe commenced the Following week, and not many weeks after she was consuming it, she began to strive a bit -I well recall the first day I saw her mom stand her up beside a wall, and she stood there for a few seconds.

Shawn was taken back to the doctor as scheduled, and her father later told me that after the doctor finished examining her, he asked if they had made any changes to her diet. Beth informed him that they had added Sprat tea to her routine. Not being aware of what Sprat tea is, he added: Well, whatever it is, keep it up, as I see a lot of positive changes in her.

Well—without going into all the painful details of how Sprat tea became a central part of Shawn's diet—I will simply say this: Shawn will be 22 years old this November, and with a deeply saddened heart, I must share that she remains as helpless as a three-month-old. The only thing she can do for herself is sit up on her own—one of the few skills she gained while she was drinking the Sprat tea. I have and will continue to pray for her, but I often wonder if she will remain this way for the balance of her life, or was she born for a greater purpose?

Experienced and written by: Corine V. Solomon

"Fought to Live"

Our Third Son Geoffrey's birth was delayed by almost two weeks, and at birth it was very evident that he had lost a lot of weight -as his little frail body on both of his lower sides opposite his Pelvis was what seemed to be two large cuts that seemed to be healed leaving bad scars.

The doctors told us the scars were caused by his unborn struggle to live and in so doing he had obtained hernias, but that he could not undergo surgery until he was much older, as he had also consumed fluids and mucus in the birth channel, thereby he had developed asthma.

For years, we struggled with the pain of watching our son suffer from these ailments. Many times, we were terrified at the thought of losing him. Finally, the surgery was over—but still, he often suffered terrible asthma attacks. By the time he was about seven years old, I had heard many testimonies about God healing the sick. I decided I would ask Him to please heal Geoffrey of asthma. I prayed, and to my surprise, the attacks stopped for weeks.

Then one night, just before I went to bed, I did my usual check on the children. As I walked out of the boys' bedroom, I suddenly heard the familiar sound of wheezing—Geoffrey was struggling to breathe again. In great passion and faith, I cried out and commanded the devil in the name of Jesus Christ to leave my son alone. Instantly, the wheezing stopped. And from that night on—praise God—the asthma never returned.

As an adolescent, Geoffrey met a boy from Jamaica that was around his age who was an asthmatic as he was -Geoffrey shared his healing story with the boy, telling him to go ask me to pray to Jesus for him, and assured him that Jesus would heal him. This is yet another testimony of God's mercy. my mind reflects on the scripture in Matthew 18, 3 where Jesus told his disciples that unless we become as a little child, we will not enter the kingdom of God.

Geoffrey, even since becoming an adult -I have never heard him say that he had ever had any attack from asthma.

Praise God for all of His blessings towards my family and I.

What He has done He will do again.

Experienced and written by: Corine V. Solomon

"Five Days of Rain"

In August 2016, we experienced a five-day stretch of low-grade tropical storms—what some referred to as trenching rains. The exact day or date escapes me now, and that absence troubles me. Like so many other blessings God has graciously bestowed upon me, this moment has faded into a blur. I often regret having given up the practice of keeping a diary or journal, for had I continued, I would now hold the precise details I long for. I've always valued truth in all I do, and memory, when left uncultivated, becomes unreliable. As the old saying goes: "If you don't use it, you'll lose it." Any way Thank God, I recall what matters: at that time, it was just my husband and I at home when the heavy rains started just after breakfast, it had been raining for just a short while when we noticed a thin stream of water draining down the wall of the passage way that leads to our bedroom. This caused us to search the house to see if there were any more leaks, and in so doing, we learned that both of our bathrooms, and two out of the other three bedrooms were leaking. One of the bedrooms was worse than the other -it was what we call pouring water.

The rains became heavier with the passing time.

We labored as best and as fast as we could trying to secure the Mattresses of the Beds from destruction, we worked in relay mopping water, and emptying the many Pails we had set to catch water, and soon we were becoming too tired to go on any longer.

On one of my trips back from the laundry room, carrying the mop, pail, and rags, I approached the water cooler—which at the time stood in the pantry way. Just then, I heard the quiet voice of the Spirit gently reminding me that He was with us. Moved by this sudden reassurance, I set the items down on the floor and wrapped my arms around the five-gallon bottle resting on the cooler. With rain pounding heavily on our rooftop, I lifted my voice above the storm and cried out:

"Lord, help! We need you—please stop the leak in our house. "I collected the stuff and went on my way to the Bedroom that was leaking the worst. it was still raining heavily, but there was no water coming down from the Ceiling. seeing this, we checked all the other areas of the house that were leaking, and the water had also stopped there.

We thanked God, and I went into the Kitchen to prepare a late lunch. standing at the sink, I caught sight of my husband peeping into the Bedroom. I then asked him: "Hon, what is he saying to you?" Of course, he knew that the "he" I spoke of was the devil.

My husband replied to me: "he said that the leak has stopped because of the shift of the wind." "He was always a Liar from his beginning, and always will be, and you will see Hon," I replied.

On the second day of the storm, there was still no sign of it letting up. Yet, as we kept ourselves busy through the mid-morning, the winds began shifting—first in one direction, then another, almost as if taking turns. My husband noticed it and commented on the pattern. I turned to him and said, "So, hon—if it was the shift in the wind yesterday that caused the leak to stop, then what's the reason the house isn't leaking now? "We rejoiced and gave God thanks for His Blessing to us.

The rains ended on the fifth day, and our house never again leaked.

Weeks later, we had a Carpenter check the housetop; he and his team found that nine sheets of the Zinc were rusted beyond repair.

Then we told them the Miracle God had done for us in the recent Storm, and the chief Carpenter said: "That is impossible." I replied: "The God we serve specializes in the impossible.

Experienced and written by: Corine V. Solomon

"Incest"

One Sunday, I think it was in 1997, my family and I went to the tabernacle for worship.

Sunday School had just ended, and people were beginning to arrive for the eleven o'clock worship service. Among those entering the Tabernacle was a father with his young daughter—she looked to be about eight years old, though she carried herself with the poise and presence of someone closer to twelve. They sat in the last seat in the back of the same section of benches where my family and I were sitting, and as they sat something happened to me that I am not aware of ever happening before: I was drawn to turn and look towards the back, and that is how I saw them taking their seat.

Among the many people entering, my attention—though I couldn't explain why at the time—briefly settled on the father and daughter. It was only for a moment, but it felt significant. I quickly turned my focus back to the posture of worship. And just as I did, I distinctly heard the word "incest" whispered—not aloud, but in my soul. It was so clear, it felt as though someone had leaned in and whispered it directly into my ear. A strong, almost overwhelming urge rose within me to speak the word aloud, to let others hear it too. Deep within, I knew exactly who the word was pointing to. But before I could react, the Moderator stepped forward and opened the service. I remained seated, silent, and deeply contemplative about what had just occurred.

Was I before God in error for not speaking, or was I being respectful to the service?

A few weeks later, during another Sunday service—this time the mid-morning worship had already begun—my family and I were seated in our usual seats. As the service continued, that same father and daughter entered the Tabernacle and made their way to the very first bench on the opposite side from where we sat. As they passed by me, the same word—"incest"—was whispered into my spirit just as clearly as it had been that first Sunday. Once again, I felt the strong urge to speak out against it. And once again, I remained silent. In that moment, I found myself wondering: Am I committing the sin of omission?

So, what did I do about this matter? I surrendered it all to God. I asked Him to forgive me for not speaking out—because, just maybe, if I had obeyed His prompting, the father's freedom from sin and the little girl's suffering could have come to an end sooner.

Two years later, the unimaginable happened. The child fell ill at school, and a teacher rushed her to the hospital. Without going into the painful details, it was revealed that she was pregnant—just ten years old—and was losing the baby. It broke my heart when I heard that she had told the doctor her father had been giving her long white capsules and castor oil.

Of course, this went to court, and I heard that the father was given twelve years imprisonment.

The rest of this story is yet to be revealed -of which it will be; I do hope and pray that this father will truly repent and surrender his life to The Lord.

Experienced and written by: Corine V. Solomon

"A Miracle off a Highway"

One busy Saturday evening in 2021, my husband and I were traveling home from the east side of the island after visiting our daughter and granddaughter. We hadn't been on the route for long when my husband fell asleep. As he rested, I turned on my audio Bible in the car's CD player, a routine I followed, especially when driving alone.

The traffic in both lanes traveling down and up was quite busy as it is most of the time on the island nowadays, especially since Hurricane Ivan in 2004.

Finally, we were crossing Hurley's supermarket, which placed us where we were almost home, and my husband was still asleep.

Reaching the junction of three way traffic, one being the road that leads to where traffic can exit into the main South road, and one onto Linford Piercy Highway, and the other that led into Crew road which was where I was to travel on to reach our home, as I took the slight turn in the lane to enter Crew Road which brought the left side of my car almost facing the road-Island that's placed right in the middle of the highway at the top, which divides the ongoing and upcoming traffic.

As my car was positioned with its left side facing the island in the middle of the highway, a speeding, brilliant blue car suddenly merged around the area near the road island that faces the Silver Oaks Compound. It passed right through my car, almost like a gentle breeze, causing no damage to my husband, my car, or myself. Through the corner of my left eye, I saw that car go over the Island and down the highway, still speeding.

We reached home safely -and as I drove into our garage my husband awoke -I was still too stunned, and amazed to share what him what I had just experienced, and must admit at that time I was not quite sure how my husband would respond to my story, of which I shared with him some years later, and of course he believed me as he for years had seen some of the works of God.

From time to time, I shared this experience with others, but I still feel unsure whether anyone truly believed it. What gives me peace over time is knowing that the Holy Spirit reminded me of this event, just as He did with all the other true testimonies in this book. I am certain of how I saw His protection over my husband and me, and I also believe that He extended the same protection to the driver of the other car that Saturday evening. I am once again happy to give God thanks and Praise for all. He has done in my life, and for all. He will do before He takes me home, which will all bring Glory to His name and an extension to His Kingdom.

Thank God I have been aided in truly believing that there is not nothing that God cannot do, I pray the same for all who read and hear of the manifestation of God through and for me.

Experienced and written by: Corine V. Solomon

"The Death of a Q C"

One Sunday in 1999, my husband and I made ready to attend Worship service at the Church of God full gospel in Savannah. I happened to be the driver for the day as it was only my Car, a Grand Marquis, available.

Just before entering the main road, I noticed that my husband was not wearing his seat belt, so as we mostly all the time when we were driving, I said: Timothy, put on your seat belt, as the life you save may be your own.

We had just passed Hurleys Supermarket when I suddenly felt the presence of someone in the back seat. At that moment, I heard a whisper in my right ear, urgently saying, "Turn left, turn your head." I immediately obeyed, and out of the corner of my right eye, I saw a yellow car speeding toward us.

If I had not obeyed the command, I heard whisper to me, it would have been a direct head-on collision, as the driver had overtaken the oncoming lead of traffic.

My husband and I escaped with only some old hurts being provoked, the car was badly damaged on the right side of the front.

The case was handed over to a local lawyer, and the offers of payment from the other driver's insurance were twice refused by our lawyer. After a few months, our lawyer called me to schedule an appointment. He told me that a foreign lawyer had offered assistance with my case and that he wanted to meet with me to discuss the matter further. I was about three steps up the Staircase that led to our lawyer's Office, which I walked slowly due to my Spine Problem and my memory of a fall off the stairs in 1986.

Looking up the steps which I was to walk, I saw an elder white man standing on the balcony of the stairs and slightly leaning over the railing smoking a Cigarette, I again heard the somewhat familiar whisper which said: "That's the Lawyer, and he do not have very long to live."

Our lawyer, along with the man who was smoking the cigarette on the balcony—whom I later learned was a QC—were introduced to me by our lawyer, and I to him.

The meeting went well, and the Q C closed it by assuring our Lawyer of the amount that they would settle for me, of course plus their pay, and once again shaking hands with us.

I deliberately lingered in my seat to speak to our Lawyer in private, on seeing the Q C leave and heard him walking down the stairs. I said to our Lawyer calling him by name: "If you are going to accept the aid of the Q C with our case you have to move fast, as he will not be here very long."

Our Lawyer questioned me on what I meant by my statement, I replied to him in simple words: "He do not have very long to live." Without words Our Lawyer looked at me in wonder; I did not ever learn what crossed his mind concerning the statement -not even the day about two months later when he called me to tell me that the Q C had passed away the night before.

We were back to where we were, before the offer of help from the Q C so I told him the amount that I would accept from the insurance.

I thank and praise God for being just who He is: The Almighty I AM, and I am glad He is my all and all, and I wish always to be pleasing in His sight.

Brethren, family, and friends, He is a friend that stays closer than any faithful brother.

If you have not accepted Christ Jesus as your Savior, I admonish you to do so now, and if you have, then take another grip of His hand and pull closer to Him.

Experienced and written by: Corine Solomon

"My Brush with Death"

My Husband and I went to bed -I would guess around nine thirty. I had already woken up once, and as a habit, I always check my phone before going to the bathroom or on my way back before heading back to bed. It was after midnight, though I don't recall the exact time. What I do remember is that I fell back to sleep almost immediately. Soon after, I was awoken by a knock on my room door. As I thought about asking who it was, I was quickly admonished in my spirit not to speak. I lay still, staying quiet, listening to my husband sleep, and waiting to hear if whoever had knocked would return. I sensed that there was a presence in my room. I was not so deeply scared, but my being was a bit sort on alert.

I opened my eyes and saw a woman. I was well acquainted with standing on the left north side at the foot of my bed, as quick as I caught sight of that woman, she was gone.

I then sat up on the side of my bed, and desired to call my husband to pray with me, and keep my company; feeling not myself, I just struggled in my soul and kept on praying and thank God. I eventually fell back to sleep.

Some days later, I guess it was about a week or so; this action was replayed again after the midnight hour.

In place of the woman, there appeared to be what looked like a square block of cement, freshly made. I assumed it to be about eighteen by eighteen inches. This light silverish block was slowly floating towards me. I could clearly see the four sharp corners, one of which soon pressed against my chest, as if trying to enter. It was at that moment that I realized the block was something like hot ice. By now, I was crying out to God for help, but all I could hear coming from me were deep groans.

In all this, I made an effort to awaken my husband by flinging my righthand down on him as hard as I could -as I needed help and human company, seconds after that I was thrown to the floor against the Ottoman that was near my bay window off the north side of our bed -my husband soon reached the Ottoman lifting my head into his lap he frantically kept calling me -I kept trying to let him know that I would be OK -I being fully conscious I was aware -though not being fully mobile I knew that whatever it was that had attacked me had gone, but well knowing my husband and also that we were alone -he would need someone to be with us I did my best and told him with all the strength I had to call the Ambulance he received quick response and was taken through the usual questions.

Within just a few minutes, the ambulance arrived at our gate, and we were soon at the hospital. Throughout it all, I kept praying, desiring to remain consciously in the presence of God. I was fully aware that my words in prayer were only coming out as groans, as if I were in pain.

One of the nurses on duty rebuked me for groaning, informing me that there were other people in the hospital. I wished so much that I was able to explain to her that I was praying, but I was not.

The Doctor ran the usual check, and reported his finding "All test are normal." which was no surprise to me as I knew that this was not from the physical, but of the spiritual; and after all I went to the hospital only because I wanted my husband to have company while I regained my physical strength -but I did wonder what was the reason for this attack.

I took this like all my other experiences to the Lord in Prayer – not questioning God, but asking Him a question of what was the reason for it?

As before, all the answers I received were: "So that you may help others."

Experienced and written by: Corine V. Solomon

"Three Warnings"

Although my husband always wished to be a good husband and father, his unsaved lifestyle brought much pain into our marriage and brought many enemies into my life. Yet, I thank God that we were blessed to celebrate sixty-one years of marriage in January 2024, and today, he is pressing on the upward way. Back in those years when my husband was living his riotous life, I was given a dream which occurred three times within one week, the first time in the dream, I was standing in the entrance of where I used to park my car, which caused me to be looking towards the road in the front of our home, and in the passage between our home and the road was a burnt car, and my attention was deeply drawn to take note of it.

Before my husband left for work that morning, I asked him to please get a mechanic to check the car engine, he gave me a logical excuse of why he could not have it done that day.

The second dream that week was just as the first.

Upon waking, I once again asked my husband to have the car checked. Yet again, he said he couldn't take it to the mechanic, insisting instead that the car wasn't due for its yearly servicing. I continued to plead with him—just to have the mechanic check the engine for any shortages—but once more, I lost the battle. That Friday night—or perhaps in the early hours of Saturday—the dream returned. But this time, for the third time, I saw something even more haunting: inside the burned car was a body, scorched and shriveled, charred almost to black coal. On awakening that Saturday morning -for the third time took my plea to my husband to have the car checked, he was not too pleased to have to add the checking of the car to the list of all he had planned for the day, so reluctantly he took the car for the check.

On his return from the mission of the car he was humbled as he told me that he was so glad that I had pleading with him concerning the checking of the car. I cannot fully express what he felt, but I could see he was deeply shaken, caught in a loop of disbelief. He held out the gas line that had been removed and told me what the mechanic had said—that if even a single stray spark from the engine had occurred, the car would have exploded. Driving it there could have cost him his life. The gas line had thirteen puncture holes, seemingly made with a sharp object—something like an ice pick.

Being faithful to God pays off dear ones, as He stands by His word which He honors more than he does His name -Psalms 138: 2, Isiah 54: 17.

I thank and Praise Him for being God Almighty and saving and keeping my soul.

Experienced and written by: Corine V. Solomon

"When God Says No"

Sometime in 2011, my husband began feeling unwell. Over the next few months, he was seen by several doctors, but the cause of his illness remained undiagnosed. Then one day, he heard about a visiting neurologist working at Chrisie Tomlinson Hospital. I encouraged him to see if this doctor could help, and though he was willing to try, he asked that I accompany him. He endured all the test that was required, and when they were all over the Doctor informed us that the tissue taken in the biopsy, he would be taking it to the Hospital where he worked in the USA but assured me that he would have the results back to us within a week to ten days.

Was it within the week or was it on the tenth day that I received the call from the neurologist I do not recall, but I answered the phone right away, as I was in my home office where the phone was located.

I heard the doctor's voice on the other end requesting to speak to me, I assured him that it was I who was speaking to him.

Identifying himself, he said: "Mrs. Solomon, I have some good news and some bad news for you, which would you prefer first?"

"Well -let's get the bad out of the way first," I replied. He then said: "Well, I regret to tell you that your husband has Prostate Cancer, and it is aggressive." I was stunned into speechlessness for a while, but recomposing myself, I asked: "Well medically, what is the time limit with that?" What I meant was: the Cancer being aggressive, how long medically will be estimated for him to live.

The doctor responded with compassion, yet without delay: "Three to four months. But please, allow me to share the good news." Without hesitation, he continued, "I can help with that. There are three options I can offer that may help prolong life: surgery, chemotherapy, and chemo seeds." He then went on to explain each of the three options.Just as I placed the phone on its hook, and pushed my office chair away from the desk, I heard the spirit say: "Go Pray for him, but do not tell him anything concerning the Cancer being aggressive."

I found him and a friend of his chatting in the garage -Interrupting their conversation: I greeted his friend -and promptly asked him if he believe that God can heal people from sickness and diseases, he said that he did, but I again asked him if he truly did, and he assured me that he did.

I then turned to my husband and informed him of the test results the doctor had shared—everything, except the part about it being aggressive cancer. I then informed him of what the spirit told me concerning praying for him and asked them to please let us get reverent before God, reminding them of what the word says in Matthew 18: 19 concerning if two or three are gathered in His name.

I well recall placing my left hand on my husband's shoulder -for no other reason but to make bodily contact in Prayer, I asked God if it was His will to please heal him.

After the prayer, I explained to my husband's friend why I had questioned him so deeply about his belief in God's healing. I then shared the story from Mark 5:21–43, where Jesus raised a young girl from the dead, and pointed out that He had put out of the room those who did not believe in Him. The appointed time for the doctor to return to the Island was granted, and my husband's appointment was scheduled for the following day.

The doctor informed us of the three options of help he had to offer, and waited patiently for some time on our response, my husband was struggling to decide, so the doctor asked me if I had a decision.

"I would prefer, if any, that he try the chemo seeds, but after all, he has the last say in the decision," I replied.

My husband agreed and within the week he was in and out of hospital.

Much since then has taken place with my husband health since then, but one day a few Years after he had started taking some special injections every three Months for the Prostate.

In our conversation that day, he told me that he believes that he was healed the day we prayed in the Garage.

I then asked him, "If you believe you are healed, why do you continue taking the injections?" But in that very moment, I was instantly checked in my spirit for asking such a question. Something profound was revealed to me—an understanding in the spirit about the depth of human weakness. I than asked him to forgive me for that question and went on to tell him that I understood -yet at that time I was unable to fully explain the reason I understood.

Twelve years have passed since my husband was diagnosed with aggressive cancer, and given three or four months to live. It is plain to see that even in the face of death, things can change—when God says no.

Experienced and written by: Corine V. Solomon

"Curious to see Satan"

I was young in the faith, having been saved for only about three or four years. when I heard it said that Satan/the Devil was once the most beautiful Angel in God's Heaven, and some said that he had power next to God.

Exactly which of these stories caused my Curiosity to rise so high that I desired to see him - I am not sure it may have been both, but this desire grew to such an extent that I began asking God to show him to me.

I guess it was for quite a few months after I began to place this request to God, when we as a family had to take a young man in as if he was long lost family. He was a stranger to us. He too was from Honduras the country of my birth -but from a part of the country I had not even heard of until I met with him, he being a young adult with responsibilities, and needed to earn a living my husband and I did our best to give him some days work.

One of the days that he was working around the yard, my husband had gone to work, the eldest children were all in school, leaving me and my youngest son at home.

Break time from the morning's work had arrived when the young man appeared at the back door of our home. He stretched himself out on the floor of the back porch. Seeing him there, I offered him a glass of water. As he took it from my hand, he looked at me and said, "Sister, don't ever pray to see the Devil."

His words left me speechless.

Anyone could understand why I was so taken aback—because, though I had never told a soul, not even my husband, that I had indeed whispered such a dangerous prayer. I had asked God to let me see Satan. And now, here was a stranger, speaking directly to my hidden thoughts. I stood there in stunned silence, turning his words over and over in my mind, unsure whether to feel fear, shame, or wonder.

Well -it was just a few days after the young man had warned me not to pray to see the Devil, when before day one of my son came to our bedroom very sick with high favor His body was so hot that we were not able to allow him to sleep between his Dad and I, so I asked his Dad to take the floor bed for the balance of the night, which he spread beside the left side of our bed, I had our son move over to where his Dad were -as despite all I had did to get the fever broken -the heat from his body was too much for me to endure.

I am not sure of the exact hour in the early morning that it was, but I know that the Sun was far from rising.

My husband and son were asleep, and I lay in bed listening to the silence. The door to our bedroom was locked—I had made sure of it after letting our son in, securing the latch myself. And yet, without the door opening, without a sound, a towering, dark figure entered the room.

He was massive—masculine in form, his head nearly brushing the ceiling. He walked slowly to the foot of our bed and stood there, staring directly at me. His eyes never left mine as he spoke in a deep, hoarse voice. Then he pointed downward at my sleeping husband and commanded, "Kill him."

The moment I heard those words; I knew in my spirit who he was. There was no doubt. The air itself seemed to freeze. He was not just after my husband—he wanted our son too. Yes, it was the Devil himself.

But I was not silent. I called out, firm and unshaken: "In the name of Christ Jesus, Satan, leave my room."

In that instant, like a flash, he transformed—his figure slithered into that of a snake. He darted beneath the window curtains. To this day, I can still see the fabric's pattern clearly in my mind. Somehow, I found the strength to rise and look behind those curtains. But there was nothing—only the screen and the glass of the window, just as they had always been.

The following day I recalled what the young man had told me concerning not Praying to see the Devil, but despite that I do believe that-God had granted me the answer to that Prayer for more than one purpose: the lesson I needed at that time and to prepare me for the years that was to come.

Experienced and written by: Corine V. Solomon

"Helper Beguiled"

Our third helper came to live with us in 1994, and due to sickness, she left to return to her home and family in Jamaica in 2008. However, two years earlier, she had met a man from her country who told her that he loved her and wished to marry her. The tale of her love offer was told to me by her sometime later. One day I shared with her my need for someone to weed my Yard and asked her if she by chance know of anyone that I may get to do the Job, this I asked her in that manner as she was not one for going out often and when she did, I knew her company was limited.

Seeing that she would, at least once or twice a week after work, inform me that she was going down the road to visit her friend, I eventually spoke with her after this routine had continued for a few months. I told her that I thought it would be better for her in every way if he came to visit her instead. I suggested that she could invite him over, assuring her that his visit would be welcomed by both my husband and me. I also added that, if she wished, they could use either our chat garden or the lakeside garden area as their meeting place.

I never ever learned if she had shared the visitation offer with him, and never did she share his name with me – so I nick-named him "down the road" because every time she would be going to visit him, she would say: I am going down the road.

Some days after my chat with her concerning the need of getting someone to weed my yard, she assured me that she was not acquainted with anyone that she knew could do the job, but that she would ask her friend who lived down the road from us.

A few days later, she told me that he said that he would take the Job, she being well aware of exactly what I was expecting to be done -the day he came, she was able to deal with him concerning the Job.

Sometime during the midmorning, I left the house to go into the yard— for what reason exactly, I no longer recall. But as I stepped onto the porch, I saw a man weeding the right side of my front yard along the walkway. I assumed he was my helper's friend from down the road. I couldn't see his features clearly, as he was wearing a bedside lamp shade over his head. I stood there long enough to greet him with a "Good day." He did reply, but without acknowledging me directly. And while I stood there speaking to him, I received a message in my spirit meant for her. I am confident I can say I prayed, and thought about it before sharing the message with her - I am confident of praying, because I thank God! I can say that I pray about everything, but I am not in full memory of what exactly my words were to God concerning her situation, but as always, I am sure I asked His will to be done.

The message was that he was planning to marry her, yes, but it was not for love, but only convenience.

I am not aware of exactly how she took the message; but I did sense that after hearing it that she was dealing with a question.

A few days after Christmas that same year, and just a few months after I had shared the message with her, she told me that he had asked her to go ahead and order her wedding dress to be made in Jamaica, along with anything else she wanted for the wedding. He had promised to repay her for whatever she spent once they were there to get married. She explained that his sister was the one managing his money and that she lived in another parish, far from where her own family lived. She went on to say that her mother had already arranged for the dress to be made, using a well-fitting one she had left at home as a reference, and that she was planning to follow through with everything he had told her to do.

She went on to tell me that they had shared what they wished as a gift from each other for Christmas, his was a special Bible and hers was a reasonable cell phone and that she had saved up and purchased the Bible he wanted, and had taken it with her when she visited him on Christmas day, and when she gave him his gift he told her that he did not get hers because: well right now; I do not recall the excuse story that he gave her concerning what she wished for Christmas, but she said he went on to tell her that they would go out to Kirks Perfumery store in town, so that lifted her spirit because she love perfume and was sure he would purchase a nice one for her.

She went on to share the excitement she had felt when he was happily testing different samples of perfume. He eventually purchased a beautiful one and let her smell it. When they reached his car, she thought he was going to give it to her. As she waited for him to hand it over and wish her a Merry Christmas, he instead sprayed some inside the car and announced that he had bought it for his vehicle.

It was then, she said, that her eyes were fully opened to his true intentions, and also to God's disapproval of the plan for their marriage. A few days later, she ended the relationship. She told him how much she had spent on the dress and all the preparations for the wedding, reminding him that he had instructed her to do so and had promised to repay her. She then told me that he responded by saying he had just found out that his sister had stolen all of his money All of his money thanks and Praise to God for helping her to be only beguiled but not destroyed.

Experienced and written by: Corine V. Solomon

"A Secret"

The wife of one of my brothers had been having health problems for quite a few Years, off and on threw out the years she was in and out of the local hospital a few times, and after some time a doctor here referred her to a hospital in Miami Florida where she spent some months, she was visited twice by a few of her family members, who thought that she would be discharged very shortly.

One day my nephew her eldest son who was living in our bungalow for a few months -was hired to work in our yard with my husband and I, it was quite some time after Lunch, and the appointed time for us to quit for the day was drawing near and the three of us was working on the last section of our property.

My nephew was working off to my right about forty feet in the Northeast section of our property, and my husband and I were in the Northwest section. The seats we used were empty five-gallon pails turned upside down as they were light weight made our moving easy as we weeded.

There was a conversation taking place between my husband and me. I don't recall the exact topic, but gradually, I found myself unable to understand what my husband was saying. Instead, I heard another voice, clearly stating: "They just killed your sister-in-law." Of course, her name was used in place of where I've written "sister-in-law. I stopped weeding and looked towards my nephew. After gazing at him for a moment, I called out to him by name, asking when he had last heard from his mother. He walked over to me and shared what he had last heard, expressing how much he wanted to visit her but that he didn't have a US visa. I then informed him that he could get a waiver. I then wish that I could have shared with him what I was just told, but I could in no way share the news with him, as I too struggled with it pondering if it was real or was it just a thought caused because I was getting tired, or was it words from the enemy of our soul?

It was minutes to four in the evening, and my nephew had gathered up our tools and was headed towards the house.

I then restrained my husband and whispered to him what I had been told about the death of my sister-in-law. But before we could say anything more, my nephew's phone rang. By that time, we were in the main yard, almost beside him, when he cried out, telling us that he had just received the news that his mother had passed away only a short while ago. This secret I had never shared with anyone before except my husband.

A few days later, I learned that the medical report concerning her death was that her blood pressure went too low, and they could not get it up -but I know that they did not try to elevate her blood pressure -for exactly what reason they did not; I do not know.

But I am sure God knows about it all.

Experienced and written by: Corine V. Solomon

"Why me?"

SHORT SYNOPSIS OF MY ORIGIN

My parents were both born in the Cayman Islands, as their four parents were migrants from Germany and Ireland who had settled there. When they were babies, my mom and dad were taken to the Bay Islands of Spanish Honduras by their parents, who, like many others at the time, were seeking a better life. As a result of this move by my four grandparents, I was born in the Bay Islands of Guanaja, Spanish Honduras.

MY BIRTH

Mom told me that her mother and the mid-wife were the first two persons in this world to see my face, but assure me that long before that occurred, they both made sure that the room where my birth took place was free of everyone else, and that not even the sea breeze which always graces the low Cay were able to seep in through the seams of her little wooden house.

A SURPRISE

My birth had only just begun, lying on a floor bed that was meant to offer a bit more comfort during my mother's ordeal, when the nurse announced that I was coming feet first. Mom later told me that my grandmother shared a story with her that day. She explained that shortly after I took my first breath, a large black cat appeared at the bedroom door. It made a leap from the direction of the closed door, seemingly aiming to perch near me. In response, my grandmother did the same and blocked its path. The cat quickly changed direction and headed toward the bathroom.

Mom said that my grandmother searched the entire house for the cat, though both she and the nurse reassured me that there had been no such cat in the room, nor were they aware of any such animal in the community. Mom also mentioned that the cat was never seen again in the house, and as far as the neighbors knew, no one had ever seen such a cat in the community, either before or after that incident.

Anyway, Mom told me that my grandmother took me and dedicated me to God.

The story of my life is quite a lengthy one, but I am persuaded that anything in it that will not directly contribute to bringing glory to God and his Kingdom. I feel it fit to avoid here in, and if I tried to tell all that I can recall, it would be a very large book.

LEADANCE AND PROTECTION

I was about four years old when a tall, Black girl, whom I considered my best friend, came to visit me. I suspected she was around ten or twelve years old. She lived at the farthest point of the low Cay in Guanaja, which we called home. This friend of mine came to my parents' house to look for me, as she had done many times before. As she was leaving, she whispered to me, "Do you wish to go with me to get some cherries?" I quietly slipped away from my mother and home and went with her.

We arrived at a house painted gray with white trim. At the end of the house, which faced west, there was a half door, with the top half open. A good distance from the house, I saw a big canoe under a coconut tree. Peeking from the north corner of the house was a cherry tree limb weighed down with red cherries—something I noticed as my friend stopped by the lean-to opposite the house.

She told me not to follow her but to wait for her by the lean-to. I obeyed, keeping my eyes on her as she arched her back and snuck through the bottom half of the door, heading toward the cherry tree. Just as she reached the tree, the bottom half of the door suddenly swung open. A large boy ran out, grabbed my friend, but she freed herself from his grip and began to run toward the canoe. I then saw the boy pick up a large brown object, which I thought was a dried coconut, and throw it at her, hitting her in the back of the head. She fell into the canoe, and he pursued her. I immediately began running home as fast as my little legs could carry me.

The next morning, I heard that she was missing, but I didn't reveal what I had seen the day before. It wasn't until about twenty-five years later that I shared what I knew, and I will explain later how God's mercy was with me that day.

In the years before that secret was revealed, I went through many experiences, but as mentioned before, I will share only those that directly bring glory to God.

December Nineteen, fifty-four, our mom took my two brothers and me to the nearby beach. She took an adult straw basket, my brothers had theirs. I had the paint can that mom had cleaned and placed a handle on for me to back water and the like, from this beach mom gather the white sand for our yard -as she by then were adjusting to the customs of the Islanders and she needed the white sand to make our yard white for Christmas.

Having not seen the sea for such a long time, I was eager and tempted to sneak in and take a bath. Back home in Guanaja, I could do that anytime I wished, as all the homes there were built on the shallow reefs. Many areas had pools or "white holes," some formed by nature and others crafted by the skilled hands of devoted grandfathers and fathers. They did this so that the children could always have shallow waters to bathe in. I assumed this was where I was sneaking into, but I was soon greatly surprised when I slipped off a ledge into deep water, which seemed to be slowly swallowing me.

I fought, using my dog paddle stroke, to get to the surface. I managed to do this twice, and on my second time up, I caught sight of my youngest brother, Watson, who was two years older than me. He was running toward me, yelling, "Coring is drowning, mama!" I knew it was Jesus who had sent him to help me, though at that time I didn't understand it was the Holy Spirit who had nudged him to look toward the sea when they realized I was missing from their company. They had been busy filling their baskets.

Ever since that day, Watson became my earthly protector, remaining so until just before I got married.

Some time later, I was invited by two girls to go with them to a water hole to bathe. Once again, I didn't get permission from either of my parents, and I knew full well that I was doing something wrong. The rule was that we children were always supposed to get permission from at least one of our parents, but I still took my bike and went on my merry way with the girls, both of whom were older than me.

When we reached the big water hole, I knew, deep in my mind, that I shouldn't go in. Despite the pressure I felt from the two girls, I resisted for a while. However, the younger of the two, whom I had chosen as my friend, climbed into the water and tempted me to join her. Eventually, I gave in to the temptation. But I quickly realized that the water hole was much deeper than the "white holes" back home.

As I struggled to make my way out of the deep water, I noticed that the two girls were mocking my distress. Even the girl who was in the water with me didn't offer to help. In my efforts to escape, I swam with a dog paddle and finally reached the side of the hole. But there was nothing to grip onto to pull myself out. I pressed my hands as hard as I could on the earth at the edge of the hole and tried to use my feet to gain traction on the smooth wall. It seemed impossible, until I suddenly felt different levels of shelves protruding from the wall. I was able to climb up on them and pull myself out.

Once out of the water, I saw that the girls were staring at each other in surprise and disappointment. I knew immediately that I needed to distance myself from their company. I grabbed my bike from the ground and pedaled home as fast as I could.

Then, as the early years of my life continued, I later learned and understood that God was guiding, leading, and protecting my life. A few of my childhood experiences can be read here in my book Manifestations of God, for in and through me I will not reiterate them -but you can read them if you haven't before The titles are: A man at the door, A view of the future, Poisoned…

USED BY GOD

Some time before my experience of being poisoned, I was seven years old when I started having pains that I described to my mom as stomach pain. However, after being examined by Dr. Shoecare, it was revealed that the pain was actually in my chest. After various tests, it was discovered that my heart was severely enlarged. The doctor told my mom that my heart was the size of a fourteen-year-old's. He also said that if I lived until I was thirteen, I would probably make it to adulthood.

The ordeal I endured due to my heart condition as a child is too lengthy to detail at this moment, but I must share an experience my mom had during one of the episodes I suffered. She told me this story when I was a teenager: One day, as she watched over me while I was in the midst of a spell, she became aware that we were not alone in the room. Although she felt no fear, she turned to see who was with us. Standing in front of the bureau, she saw someone she took to be Jesus. He was looking intently down at me with His arms outstretched. She said that she asked Him, "Please don't take her now, leave her with my mom." From that day onward, I began to improve. Slowly but surely, a change started to take place in her life, and it gradually extended into my dad's life as well. It took years, but I did not see the full transformation until it was almost time for them to leave this world. Thank God, though, that I was able to witness some of that change in their lives and hear their testimonies of receiving salvation.

Years before my parents' passing, since my first home was close to theirs, I hurried over to their house to share a memory I had just recalled from my early childhood. I didn't realize Dad was home until I reached the kitchen where Mom was. After greeting them, I eagerly began to share my memory.

"Dad, Mom," I said, excitedly, hoping to capture their attention. "I want to tell you both something that happened when I was little. I don't remember the people's names, but I remember that the girl's mother had four babies at once. They lived in Fire Point, and their oldest daughter went missing. She was found the next day on the little beach in Hogh Cay. They said that she had drowned."

It was then, twenty-five years later, that I told my parents the story of my tall Negro friend and the day I went with her to get cherries.

My parents then told me the names of the girl's parents. Dad said, "Well, child, it was a good thing you kept that story to yourself and had the sense to run. Had you spoken about it or if they had seen you watching, you too would probably not be alive."

Mom exclaimed, "So, that's why they sent their son off to the United States! And not many days after her death, he killed her!" Yes, I remember that when they took her body to the town's registered nurse, she examined it and told the parents that she did not drown because there was no water in her lungs.

I thank God for always giving His angels charge over me—then, now, and I trust He will forever more. All because He first loved me, I surrendered my life to Him. Yes, I still experience troubles of different kinds and magnitudes, but thanks, praise, and glory to His holy name, He always brings me through them. As His word says, "No weapon formed against thee (meaning His children) shall prosper." He has not promised that we will not be attacked, but He has promised that the evil plan will not be successful.

I admonish you, dear one, to accept Christ Jesus as your Lord and savior. Trust Him; He saves those who call upon Him, and keeps them. He will never leave or forsake. His Children, but always remember: He will not work in our life any farther than we will allow Him…

Experienced and written by: Corine V. Solomon